DRAW UP A CHAIR:

A Treasury of Renfrew County Storytelling

Published by

GENERAL STORE
PUBLISHING HOUSE

Box 28, 1694B Burnstown Road, Burnstown, Ontario, Canada K0J 1G0
Telephone (613) 432-7697 or 1-800-465-6072

ISBN 1-894263-52-9
Printed and bound in Canada

Cover and design layout by Derek McEwen

General Store Publishing House
Burnstown, Ontario, Canada

National Library of Canada Cataloguing in Publication Data

Main entry under title:

Draw up a chair : a treasury of Renfrew County storytelling

ISBN 1-894263-52-9

1. Renfrew (Ont. : County)–Anecdotes. 2. Renfrew (Ont. : County)–History. I. Code, Susan, 1960-

FC3095.R4D73 2001 971.3'81 C2001-903559-4
F1059.R4D73 2001

Cover Photos: First council for the County of Renfrew, 1897–98. Courtesy of Isabel Chanonhouse Hargreaves, great-granddaughter of the first warden, Dr. John Chanonhouse. Insert left: Wilno Station. Courtesy of the Leonard Daly Collection. Insert centre: Martin O'Grady (1836-1920) and Catherine Daly O'Grady (1851-1943) of the O'Grady Settlement. Insert right: The Little Grey House. Courtesy of Dorothy Miller.

Draw Up A Chair:

A Treasury of Renfrew County Storytelling

Edited by Susan Code

COUNTY OF RENFREW

OFFICE OF THE
COUNTY WARDEN

9 INTERNATIONAL DRIVE
PEMBROKE, ONTARIO
K8A 6W5
(613) 735-7288
FAX: (613) 735-2081

The people of Renfrew County are born storytellers. Bring two or more together, and the coffee brewing has hardly had a chance to settle before tales are exchanged like so many tips outside the betting window on fair day.

So what better way to celebrate the start of the new millennium in Renfrew County than to invite those who know it best to spin us a yarn. With the help of General Store Publishing House in Burnstown, we approached various municipal, historical, tourism, school, church, and social organizations in Renfrew County, as well as the general public, and asked them to share their stories. We wanted to compile an anthology that would highlight the people, places, and events of Renfrew County from its origins to the present.

And you did not disappoint us.

DRAW UP A CHAIR: A Treasury of Renfrew County Storytelling is a rich compendium of tales that captures the spirit of the Ottawa Valley over the last four centuries. The nearly thirty contributors have written about the lumber trade, the military, their communities, historic and fascinating people, getting about, and getting ahead. We've also included some observations on the area by those who had passed by long before (but were sure would want to be included).

The result is a fitting tribute to those who came before, and a humble gift to those yet to be.

So draw up a chair, and pour a mug of your favourite beverage, then settle back for a spell of fine tales spun about and by the people of Renfrew County.

Barry Moran
Warden

Table of Contents

Have You Ever Been To . . .

Thems That Be About

It Was This Way, So It Was

No. 23 VOL. XX.

The Canada Gazette.

PUBLISHED BY AUTHORITY

QUEBEC, SATURDAY, JUNE 8, 1861

PROVINCE OF CANADA. } EDMUND HEAD.

JOHN A. MACDONALD, *Atty. Genl.*

VICTORIA, by the Grace of God, of the United Kingdom of Great Britain and Ireland, Queen, Defender of the Faith, &c., &c., &c.

To all to whom these presents shall come or whom the same may concern—GREETING:

WHEREAS in and by an Act of the Legislature of this Province, made and passed in the Twenty-fourth year of Our Reign, intituled: "An Act to provide for the separation of the County of Renfrew from the County of Lanark," it is amongst other things enacted, that "the Reeves and Deputy Reeves of the several Townships and other Municipalities in the County of Renfrew, shall form a Provisional Municipal Council for the said county, and shall, with respect to the said County, have, possess and exercise all and singular the rights, powers, privileges and duties conferred, granted or imposed by the Laws of this Province upon Provisional Municipal Councils constituted by Proclamation, under the authority of chapter Fifty-four of the Consolidated Statutes for Upper Canada; and Our Governor in Council shall issue a Proclamation appointing a time and place for the first meeting of the said Provisional Council, and therein name one of its Members to preside at the Meeting." Now KNOW YE, that by virtue of the powers conferred in and by the above Act, and in pursuance of any other power in this behalf, Us enabling, We do by this Our Royal Proclamation, appoint THURSDAY, the TWENTIETH day of JUNE instant, as the time, and the Village of Renfrew, in the County of Renfrew, as the place for the first meeting of the Provisional Municipal Council of the County of Renfrew, and that Thomas Patrick French, Esquire, one of the Members of the said Provisional Municipal Council, shall preside at the meeting thereof; Of all which Our loving subjects and all others whom these presents may concert, are hereby required to take notice and govern themselves accordingly.

IN TESTIMONY WHEREOF, We have caused these Our Letters to be made Patent, and the Great Seal of Our said Province of Canada to be hereunto affixed: WITNESS, Our right Trusty and Well-Beloved the Right Honorable Sir EDMUND WALKER HEAD, Baronet, K. C. B., one of Our Most Honorable Privy Council, Governor General of British North America, and Captain General and Governer in Chief in an over Our Provinces of Canada, Nova Scotia, New Brunswick, and the Island of Prince Edward and Vice Admiral of the same, &c., &c., &c. At Our Government House, at Our CITY of QUEBEC, in Our said Province, this SIXTH day of JUNE, in the year of Our Lord, one thousand eight hundred and sixty-one, and in the Twenty-fourth year of Our Reign.

By Command,
CHARLES ALLEYN, Secretary.

OUT FROM HOME

Bronis' Team

by Bronis Visutskie as told to Barney McCaffrey

In the Omarnique lumber camp, along the
Bonnechere,
Bronis Visutskie of Wilno, he was a teamster
there.
Working all day and into the night, taking care
of his team and treating them right.

Come along Flossie, come on Peg, come on now,
let's shake a leg.
Come on Peggy, come along Floss, come on
now, you're a good old horse.

One morning in the lumber camp along the
Bonnechere,
The boss was angry, the boss was mad, there
was trouble in the air.
The bulldozer was down, its battery out, with
an ice cold motor that wouldn't start.
Too far to town from the lumber camp along
the Bonnechere,
Hook up the teams we'll start that machine with
what we've got right here.
Team number one and team number two, they
tried so hard, couldn't make it move,
Now these were the teams in the lumber camp,
along the Bonnechere.
Team one and two and three and four all tried,
but they all failed
Visutskie's team's the only one now, Bronis can
you do it, does your team know how?

Well come along Flossie, come on Peg, come on
now let's shake a leg.
Come on Peggy, come along Floss, come on now
let's show the boss.

There was silence in the lumber camp along the
Bonnechere
As he hooked up the team to the dozer, standing
cold and silent there.
Come on my konichka, get yourselves set, come
on now we'll show them yet.
Those two horses pulled in the lumber camp,
along the Bonnechere
Their muscles straining, Bronis driving them
hard in the cold and frosty air.
An inch, a foot, a yard, a whirr. The motor
starts, you did it old girls!
Well good old Flossie, good old Peg, you pulled
so hard, you shook a leg.
Good old Peggy, good old Floss, you pulled that
dozer and showed the boss.

The Road
by Garry Ferguson

The Matawatchan Road ran from somewhere beyond the general store, past our house to the graveyard, then continued toward places where, my mother said, robins wintered. In my little world there was no requirement for a wider comprehension of geography.

From our kitchen window, I could look across the road to our neighbour's house near the hill over which the sun came up. No matter how hard I pressed my face against the glass, my view of the road was limited to the brow of the hill near our gate and, in the direction of the store, to the knoll in front of my grandmother's house.

There would come a morning, after late autumn winds had ripped the last coloured leaves from trees, when I would wake up to a pervading silence. It was as though an enormous down comforter had covered our house, smothering all sounds from the outside world. I knew, even before I ran to look, that the first snow had fallen. In contrast to the surrounding countryside thrusting drab greys of rock, rail fences, nude trees and twisted brush through new snow, the road was a corridor of uninterrupted white. The old lumber trucks on these mornings seem to muffle their bark, as though in apology for tracking graffiti across nature's handiwork. If the storm lasted long enough, I would get to see the big wooden "V" plough throw up serpentine windrows as it slewed along behind three or four teams of horses.

My "farming grandparents" who lived near the graveyard came one evening, sleigh bells jangling in time to their horses' stride, and took my brother and me to a Christmas concert in the schoolhouse where we saw Santa Claus. From then until Christmas Eve, my excitement grew until I lost confidence in my ability to distinguish between sleigh bells on teams along the road and those on reindeer cantering through the night sky.

At some point during the time of short days and bitter frost, after my brother and I had broken our Christmas toys and snow had lost its magic, we began to long for those soft winds that carry a promise of thaw and the return of robins from lands beyond the graveyard. During spring's muddy season, we could no longer hear the "tinkatink" of the mailman's Model A. It was stranded, like a moth on a flysticker, in his yard until the roadbed dried and dust blew. In the meantime, he seemed to enjoy this break from driving, lounging on the buggy seat while his glum old horse picked its way through washouts and mud holes. We hated that horse because of its uncanny ability to *always* set a course over our miniature mud dams and flood diversions.

By the time groundhogs sought out new green shoots in the ditch across from our gate, farmers had brought teams and wagons to "pay the taxes" with annual road work. From the pit at the bottom of the hill, they hauled gravel to repair wounds inflicted during winter's death throes. With rakes and shovels they performed their surgery until all scars had disappeared and the road looked trim and rejuvenated.

Through hot summers, this fresh surface became our sandbox. Though we considered it ours, we *did* give way to vehicles. The snarl of an engine or the rumble of a wagon would send us scurrying up embankments where we waved until the dust had drifted away and nothing but locusts ruined the silence. With my brother and the neighbour's boys, I prowled the ditches on the lookout for snakes. We threw stones and tried to flush groundhogs by peeing down their holes, simply because they took up residence along our road.

Images of certain events mouldering in my cache of road memories now emerge, for some reason, against only summertime backgrounds. I remember heat and rank growth along fences when the mother of each new addition to the community came trudging through the dust carrying her latest offspring. She would stop and show it off to "Oohs" and "Aahs" from my mother while my brother and I stared, tongue-tied and grinning. After each had continued on her way, my questions always forced Mother into creating some diversionary tactic in order to protect tender sensibilities from the truth concerning the source of these babies.

Funeral processions also came through the dust, but they filled me with childish dread because they carried dead people. Dead people could become ghosts. I would watch, like a mesmerized frog under the stare of a hungry snake, as the line of vehicles slithered past our gate and down the hill. I usually knew the mourners but never looked at them in case I'd feel some of the sadness that accompanies death.

The sight of a couple of cars passing our house during the course of a summer evening not only provided entertainment, but indicated that someone, somewhere, was throwing a "do." I don't recollect this pastime during winter, I suppose, because a car would be out of sight before I could dash to a window and scrape enough frost from the pane to provide a peephole.

The impression that all local boys who went to war came home in uniform during one particular summer I attribute to a memory that tends to compress series of long-past events into neat time segments. Whether to visit our neighbours, stop in for a chat with my father, or go striding past, I saw each one of them on the road before they went overseas.

We marked the passage of time during our carefree summer days only by events that interrupted play, for all other measures were as irrelevant as the places to which the road led. We did sense the turning of a seasonal clock though, when goldenrod in gaudy yellows and milkweed with bursting pods crowded onto the gravelled shoulders as though waiting for a parade to pass. The big threshing machine rattling by on its way from farm to farm reminded us that summer was slipping away. By the time the last hunter from "out front" had passed our gate with a deer carcass slung over his front fender, we were again awaiting snowfall.

Successive spring runoffs continued to ravage the road. Farmers, however, ceased to "pay the taxes" with road work even before the war became a bad memory. Traffic changed as motorized vehicles forced horses to languish on farms. The few Model A Fords and disc-wheeled Chevies were joined by many sleeker models with better window defrosters. Frost-free windshields eased the strain of winter driving by eliminating the need for drivers to open windows and lean out. Horns no longer "beeped" or made "aooka" sounds. The new models emitted multi-toned notes impossible to imitate, even when we pushed on our Adam's apples and stuck our fingers up our noses. Huge army trucks with hydraulically operated blades eventually replaced the old wooden snowplow.

By this time, I had matured beyond the stage where an unaccompanied sortie to the outhouse taxed my capabilities, but I was still not inclined to reflect on progress. Like the mud and dust of the roadbed, change was taken for granted. I was not aware that the last vestiges of an old way of life had disappeared while I was at play. It did not occur to me that this small section of a country thoroughfare was my window on the world or that people travelling along the road were participating in micro segments of an endless jumble of broader events which, when considered in retrospect, become history.

> ***"The wagons had to be strongly built as the roads [in Renfrew County] were unbelievably bad. The driver's seat was fitted with spring-poles to ease the shocks but a small, light man was in danger of being bounced off, and Charlie Pell, who answered that description, used to strap himself on."***
>
> **— Charles Macnamara, McLaughlin Brothers Lumber Company, circa1885.**

The Age of Shanks' Pony or When Transportation Consisted of Your Own Two Legs

by Bernice M. Liedtke

Travelling the roads of Renfrew County was not always as good as it is now in this twenty-first century. In the late 1800s, roads were little more than trails consisting of a sandy-gravelly surface slicing through the thick mixed forest. They climbed over steep hills, down into swamps, and over rocks as large as a two-storey house. The roads, snake-like, wound around what they couldn't go over.

The farming community in the Schutt/Palmer Rapids area of Raglan Township produced these narratives from the age of shanks' pony. These stories may remind the reader of other tales of similar circumstances.

Circa 1870s

In a little house by a cool stream, well away from the nearest road, Karl (Charlie) Marquardt humped sacks of grain onto his shoulders. The grain was some of the harvest from the small, fertile field he had painstakingly cleared of old growth trees with the help of his oxen. His destination was the mill in the village of Combermere, a mere fifteen miles away. Using shanks' pony, he hiked the winding, hilly trail with his burden on his back to have the grain ground into flour. Returning home, he carried a one-hundred-pound sack of flour on his shoulder. With a house full of youngsters, his wife Katharine (Block) couldn't run out of flour for baking that time-honoured staple, bread. The use of shanks' pony was a normal mode of transportation for this era.

Circa 1930s

Cupid's arrow found both George Marquardt and his cousin Bill Liedtke. They resided on their parents' farms in the area of the village of Schutt. Lacking wheels to pursue their true loves, two of the Brohart sisters, the smitten young men took up their shanks' pony. They walked three hours on a route that took them past Wingle School, over the Madawaska River bridge, and past Al Capone's Hill to the Brohart farm situated between Chapese Lake and Letterkenny. Of course, any courting could only happen after they had completed a full day's (dawn 'til dusk) work. The distance did not prevent the pursuing gents from seeing their sweethearts. Love finds a way.

Circa 1930s

Hydro had not found this part of Renfrew County, so a wood-burning kitchen stove was a necessity. It was used to cook all the meals, bake bread and preserve the season's bounty. It heated water for washing and bathing and, in doing so, heated part of the house as well. You can understand the urgency when a new stove was needed by a young mother. Her husband and five friends, on foot, carried this necessity of life from Bancroft over hills, through valleys, around many twists and turns to the young couple's farm near Palmer Rapids. Approximately thirty miles one way.

Circa 1940s

The use of shanks' pony is not a problem for most small children. And the means of transportation was the last thing on the mind of Murray Liedtke at the tender age of four-and-a-half years, when he followed his nine-year-old sister, Margie, through the hilly, rock-strewn forest to Wingle School on the Concession Road just east of Schutt Road. The teacher scolded, but then chose not to send him home alone or ask his sister to take him home. There was no telephone to call his parents back on the farm, and the teacher herself couldn't leave. The only alternative was to have the child stay for the day. Murray returned to school so frequently that he was enrolled in class just to keep him safe.

Wingle School closed in 1943, but the larger Cedar Grove School opened the same year, one mile north of the old school, and shanks' pony continued to be the popular mode of transportation. Our hero walked with his cousins Paul, Jack, and Doug Marquardt the two-and-three-quarter miles each school day, in all weather, through the forest or by way of the rutted track, until he acquired a two-wheeled conveyance.

Circa 1940s

Even after many Raglan Township citizens had motorized transportation, shanks' pony was still in use. One bitter cold winter day, Eddie and Murray Liedtke had been loading logs onto the family-owned truck at the end farthest from home of White/Raglan Lake, when the back axle snapped. There was not a soul to send for help and not a telephone handy. The brothers hitched up their personal shanks' ponies and hiked across the frozen water of the lake, through the bush in deep snow to home. There they loaded an axel onto a sled for the return journey. After this exertion, they still had to install the replacement axle . . . manually.

* * *

This author remembers, quite clearly, her first view of the area described in the stories above. This occurred in the late 1950s before Highway 401 made travel from the south of Ontario to the northeast so convenient. It was a long, tiring trip of seven to eight hours back then. Weary and troubled with motion sickness from the many hills and winding curves, she was enthralled by the narrow road with undergrowth and a wall of tall trees butting the edges of the pavement. Imagination took over, seeing this land as it must have been when the first settlers arrived. Long before that, the land had been quietly, skilfully used by native people for many years. In seeing the land in this way brought the stories of explorers and traders, studied in the school text books, to life. It is, maybe, 150 years that settlers have been clearing fields here. Before that, the forest, rivers and streams were home to an assortment of wild animals, fish and birds. Many of the animals and birds adapted to living within sight of the humans who have claimed this land as their own. Tourists have found this pristine land. Some hiking trails have been established so that travelling by shanks' pony is once again in favour.

Two Men, One Woman, Two Dugout Canoes

by Neil Stewart

Some years ago, Renfrew folklorist Bernie Bedore wrote a story about two men, one woman, and two dugout canoes. He had been inspired to write the story after talking with Sandy Campbell, a descendant of Renfrew's earliest settlers.

I first heard this story when I was in Grade 10. Mr. Les Anderson had assigned us the task of writing a family history. I consulted the family genealogist, my aunt Janet Carmichael. In the course of relating the long line of ancestors, Aunt Janet told me the story of her great-grandfather's tragic loss shortly after settling on the Ottawa River near Sand Point.

Archie Stewart and his young wife, Flora Patton, had arrived at Montreal in 1819. Their first son was born and registered at St. Andrew's East, Quebec. A couple of years later, the family made their way to Upper Canada, settling next to the Duncan Campbell family in a newly surveyed township on Chats Lake, a part of the Ottawa River where there were no roads and no steamboat above Chats Falls. Another son was born in 1822 and a daughter in 1824.

By 1824, the new township had been renamed McNab by Archibald McNab, Chief of the Clan McNab. He had built a large, log home and outbuildings on the Ottawa near the mouth of the Madawaska River.

On May 10, 1825, Flora Stewart died leaving Archie with three small children and only his neighbours for help. Archie wrapped Flora's body and placed it in a dugout canoe. He tied this boat to a second dugout, which he and Duncan Campbell slowly paddled four miles down river to a spot near the confluence of the Madawaska and the Ottawa. They carried the body to the top of a high bluff and buried Flora facing east, looking out over the river. It is likely that Chief McNab gave his approval to this burial because he chose this site for a community cemetery a few years later. These two neighbours made the same journey the very next year to bury Janet Campbell's body a short distance from Flora's grave.

Historians and genealogists will find these graves in the park-like setting of Arnprior's Albert Street Cemetery, not far from other early Sand Point settlers, such as lumberman Alexander McDonnell.

Archie Stewart married again in 1827 and fathered eleven more children. Descendants of the Campbell and Stewart families still own some of the original land holdings from those early days. No matter how much local history I read or hear, no image stands out more clearly in my mind than those two men paddling their crude boats down the great Ottawa River to give the body of a young mother a proper burial.

"The characteristic hospitality that distinguished our reception by the gallant chief, when in 1828 we were returning down the Ottawa, after having explored its rapids and lakes, as far up as Grand Calumet, we cannot pass over in silence. To voyageurs in the remote wilds of Canada, necessarily strangers for the time to the sweets of civilization, the unexpected comforts of a well-furnished board, and the cordiality of a Highland welcome, are blessings that fall upon the soul like dew upon the flower. . . . As we glided from the foot of the bold bank, the gay plaid and cap of the noble Gael were seen waving on the pround eminence, and the shrill notes of the piper filled the air with their wild cadences. They died away as we approached the head of the rapids. Our caps were flourished, and the flags (for our canoe was gaily decorated with them) waved in adieu, and we entered the vortex of the swift and whirling stream."

— Joseph Bouchette, Surveyor-General to William IV, on his arrival at the home of the last Laird of McNab.
McNab built a large log home at the mouth of the Madawaska, called Kinnel Lodge.

Travelling Tales

by Bernice M. Liedtke

Circa 1900s

Alvina Marquardt's kitchen was in need of a new stove for her home at Green Lake, Schutt. It was purchased in Eganville, forty-five miles away, and entailed a two-day round trip for her husband John, with a team of horses and wagon. Alvina and their children added John's chores to their normal ones for the time he had to be away.

Circa 1910

It was the custom of John Marquardt at the end of each week to currycomb the coats of his horses. Following this task, he polished the brass bells and cleaned the leather harness. Sunday morning the family climbed aboard the buggy and with the sparkling coated team and the twinkling, chiming bells set off for St. Stephen's Lutheran Church for Sunday service. This sound was especially enjoyed on a crisp, quiet morning in winter as the team and sleigh sliced through the snow.

Circa 1940

Arnold Liedtke with his youngest son Murray drove his team of horses to Palmer Rapids on an early spring day. The road, for a distance, ran beside the Madawaska River. The heavy snow and ice of the long winter along with spring rains forced the river to rise over its banks, causing the road to be awash. Gingerly, Arnold coaxed his team to walk where the road should have been. Water crept up the wheels. As it began to seep through the wagon's floorboards, Arnold and Murray scrambled to place the bags of grain on the seat to keep them dry. Safely past the flood, they carried on to town and Albert Liedtke's hammer mill.

A Frosty Tale

In the mid-1940s, the only snowplough was owned by Edward Gogolin. It consisted of a truck with a "V" blade that somewhat successfully cleared a narrow rutted path more or less in the centre of the road leaving banks of stiff snow on either side. Before the arrival of this snowplough, the roads were never ploughed. Arnold Liedtke drove the winter-frozen corduroy road between his farm just north of Schutt through Palmer Rapids often in his lifetime, both by horse then by automobile. His son, Murray, remembers one occasion he with his father were returning home in the family car from a trip to Proudfoot's store, Palmer Rapids. The rain changed to freezing rain while they shopped. Arnold needed to stop often to scrape ice from the windshield. The tires spun on the increasingly slippery surface causing the car to slip and slide on the rutted track. Gaining the top of Eddy Budarick's hill, Arnold shifted to a lower gear. He struggled to steer while his young son sat motionless, eyes bulging and petrified, awaiting the outcome.

The car took on a mind of its own as it slid downhill. It suddenly broke out of the icy rut, swung sideways, and grazed a large poplar tree on its wild ride. Arnold finally brought the car to a stop where White Lake Creek follows the culvert under the road. He climbed out to see the damage to his car, while Murray, his exuberance returned, clambered up the icy track to survey the damage to the poplar. The tree suffered a one-foot-square, deep, gaping hole while the car sustained no damage; just a chunk of bark caught in the heavy, steel bumper.

The Sand Point-Burnstown Road

by Neil Stewart

In 1847, a road had been surveyed from Sand Point to Burnstown. Leaders in the townships of McNab—such as Alexander McDonnell—Bagot, and others more remote saw this as a way to open up the country to the southwest. Since 1835, steamers had run between Chats Falls and Chenaux, stopping regularly at the Sand Point wharves. In 1850, Dugald C. McNab, using a pseudonym, wrote a letter to the editor of the *Bytown Packet* concerning the advantages of improving the Sand Point–Burnstown Road. In May 1852, James Brown, the McNab township census enumerator, wrote:

> "Another leading road but only lately opened, passes from the village of Burnstown, better known as Madawaska Bridge, to Sand Point, at the Chats Lake, a distance of a little more than 10 miles. The road from this situation, opening up the centre of the township, will when put in good repair, become a most useful thoroughfare from the upper country on the Madawaska River to the Ottawa, meeting the navigation at Sand Point."

The road cut through the north corner of Andrew Hamilton's farm on the sixth concession. In 1868, the trustees of School

Section (S.S.) No. 13 purchased property from Andrew Hamilton on which to build a schoolhouse at the intersection of the Sand Point–Burnstown Road with the seventh line. In the early 1860s, John Young and his wife Grace Hamilton sold one acre on the corner of the intersection to Daniel and Janet McAlinden. They opened a large store opposite the schoolhouse. Dan McAlinden was Irish and nicknamed Lundy, so the intersection soon became known as Lundy's Corners.

Described as a "large country store" in the census of 1891, Lundy's became a landmark for travellers going from Arnprior or Sand Point to the country southwest of McNab Township. An anecdote related by old-timers tells the time when a resident came in to pay his bill for a grinding wheel and Lundy charged what the customer thought was an extravagant price. It seems that Lundy was unable to read or write, but would draw a sketch whenever he was recording purchases. He had drawn a circle beside this person's name and explained, "I forgot to put the hole in it and I charged you for a round of cheese."

In February 1887, the New Glasgow correspondent to the *Renfrew Mercury* reported that, "Mr. Daniel Young has started a store at Lundy's Corners. Probably he is working on the principle that 'opposition is the life of trade.'" The Young store lasted until about 1920.

In 1895, Dan McAlinden died at the age of seventy-eight and his widow Janet sold the property to James Gillan Jr. In 1905, Mr. Gillan sold the property but moved the building to a lot he had bought in the village of New Glasgow from Peter McIntosh.

> ***"The Portage [at Chats Falls] is here very difficult and dangerous but only 270 paces. Here we dined in misery, nothing could prevent the Attacks of our relentless Enemies.[1] The Passage from hence after [for] two miles is through a winding channel and consists entirely in the most frightful Rapids[2], running at least ten miles an Hour over Beds of Rock. Here the skill of the Voyageurs now shows itself; at one moment using their Poles, then their paddles, then jumping into the water, now using the Tow Line which if it was to break would end in certain Destruction to all. After passing this dangerous Channel you arrive at the Lac des Chats so called from the Quantity of Raccoons which formerly filled the adjacent woods."***
>
> **— Nicholas Garry, Deputy-Governor, Hudson's Bay Company, 1821 diary entry during journey up the "Utawa."**

[1]Mosquitoes. Garry mentions mosquitoes and other insect pests twelve times in his diary between the Rideau Falls and Mattawa.
[2]Chats Rapids.

S.S. No. 13 McNab (Glasgow)
The first school was built in 1868 at the intersection of the Sand Point–Burnstown Road and the seventh line on a corner of Andrew Hamilton's farm. It was a log structure with benches for seats. When Lundy's store was built across the road in 1881, parents would get the children to carry home supplies. This school lasted until 1905 when a new brick schoolhouse was constructed in Glasgow Village on part of the McIntosh farm. The old log school was bought by the Methodists and used as a church until after World War I. It was later bought by Dan Young and used as a stable.

The first teacher in the new school was Violet Mackie, who had received her primary education in the old log school. The school bell was taken from Lundy's Corners to the new school in the village. In 1968, the Glasgow Women's Institute erected a cairn with the old bell on top to commemorate the site of the original log school.

The Boer War (1899–1901) had three local boys involved who had attended the little log schoolhouse at Lundy's Corners. They were Troopers Alex W. Stewart, Andrew H. Miller, and Amos E. Burton. Although Alex Stewart suffered a chest wound, all three returned safely to Canada.

The Independent Order of Good Templars
A lodge of the Independent Order of Good Templars (IOGT) was started at Glasgow in the 1870s. A lot was purchased from Dave Mackie in 1877 and a log building was erected for the temple across the road from the school. The main purpose of this society was the promotion of abstinence from alcoholic beverages. Although it is not clear just when the Glasgow lodge was disbanded, it is known that most lodges ceased operations during World War I. The troops overseas were given a rum ration and most of the boys found this a comfort amidst the dreary, debilitating life in the trenches. One ninety-eight-year-old veteran joked that for some members of the templars overseas, the letters IOGT meant, "I Often Get Tight."

Landmarks
On November 6, 1894, Peter McIntosh sold a lot to partners James Denny, William E. Croft, and Arthur H. Croft on the east half of Lot 19, Concession 7. There they operated a cheese factory until about 1901.

Farmers in the Glasgow and Dewar Settlement area formed a co-operative named the Glasgow and Dewar Cheese Factory Association. The farmers bought a lot from James A. Hamilton on June 28, 1901, and erected a house and factory. Milk was brought from Dewars, Lochwinnoch, Stewartville, and surrounding area.

During World War I, production costs increased then, during the 1920s, the price of cheese

Independent Order of Good Templars District Meeting, May 26, 1906.

dropped. Farmers turned the production of milk to dairy use and cream to butter. In 1927, the association sold the factory to James Cox of Pakenham. The association lasted for a few more years until the effects of the Depression brought about its demise. Mr. Cox dismantled the building and moved it to Almonte. The house was later acquired by Charles Young; it was the home of John C. Young for many years.

The intersection of the eighth concession with the Sand Point–Burnstown Road was known as "the cheese factory corner" until the building of new Highway 17.

The first Glasgow post office began in 1889 in Dan McAlinden's store. Prior to this, mail was received or sent from McNab (1839–55), Stewartville (1865–1913), Lochwinnoch (1875–1913), Burnstown (1854–present), or Sand Point (1851–1969). At first the post office was called New Glasgow, but because New Glasgow and Glasgow existed in Quebec and Nova Scotia, Ottawa insisted on a change of name. New Glasgow became Harvey Post Office, a name never really accepted by the community. The mail was carried three times each week from Arnprior by Paddy Doolan. Harvey was believed to be the name of Paddy Doolan's father.

The post office was moved to Andrew Young's home in the early 1890s. Andrew Young served as postmaster until September 1, 1902. The post office was then moved to the village and the name became Glasgow Station.

Other landmarks along or near the road were the schoolhouses at S.S. No. 7 McNab, the Presbyterian church at what became known as Dewar's Settlement, and O'Donnell's store near the eleventh line.

Of course the hill at Sand Point provided a merry ride for teamsters trying to negotiate the sharp turn with a heavy load on a wagon or sleigh. On more than one occasion, teams were known to lose control and loads slid down the hill and over top of the sheds below.

From 1835 to 1873, when the railway was completed to Renfrew, Sand Point was one of the most important centres in south Renfrew. Old-timers from Renfrew, Bagot, Brougham, Griffith, and Matawatchan used to tell stories of their arrival at Montreal and how they made their way by steamers up the Ottawa. Baggage and goods were transferred at the various rapids and falls to the next steamer, finally arriving in Sand Point. Then, they continued their long and arduous journey to their destination in one of the interior townships.

Sand Point had inns from the very earliest times and, by the end of the nineteenth century, had a very good stopping place in Young's Hotel.

There were stores and a couple of factories, but the most thriving entrepreneur of the early days was Alexander McDonnell. His imposing stone home still stands near the start of this historic road.

At the southwest end of the road, Burnstown became an important destination point for the log drives on the Madawaska. It also had inns, stores, a school, and a church. Several of the old buildings have been restored or renovated, and are still useful, functioning places of commerce.

When we travel along the Calabogie Road, McLean Drive, or the Golf Club Road in the Township of McNab/Braeside, most of us never think of those early days and what that road would have meant to the development of our area in the mid and latter parts of the nineteenth century. Perhaps we should take a moment now and again to consider what we owe to our pioneer ancestors.

Learning to Drive

by Elaine Mundt

The year was 1949. Dad had given me permission to drive his truck. Learning to drive a vehicle had been topmost in my mind since I was nine. I had watched my Dad, Len Knuth, and his brother, my Uncle Harold, start the truck that went to the railroad station in Golden Lake twice a day, five days a week. Naturally, I had to go along to watch the trains come in to the station—one from Ottawa going to Whitney, and one from Pembroke. My dad operated the post office, so a trip to the station to take the mail and receive the mail was a regular routine. It has been proven that this was the best postal service ever because when the bags of mail were placed on the train, postal workers on the train sorted the mail in the mail car, bagged it, and there the mail was ready for dispatch as the train stopped at each station along the way.

Anyway, sometimes on these trips my uncle would let me steer the truck.

But in order to drive, I had to know how the clutch worked on the truck and how to shift gears. I would sit in the parked vehicle and try out all the pedals and the gear shift, and pretend that I was driving to unknown places. I was confident that this was all I needed to know to get started on my driving career.

The truck the author learned how to drive on.
Photo courtesy of Elaine Mundt.

Dad handed me the keys.

"You can drive only in our yard," he said.

Our yard had a street frontage and the only way back was up a slight elevation to the outhouse. So there I was, between a street and an outhouse! I was twelve years old and quite short in stature. It was hard to press down the clutch with my left foot, press the brake with my right foot, and start the truck. But, there it went, and I was in control. I put the gear in reverse, took my foot off the brake, pressed the gas pedal, and released the clutch. The truck jerked forward, not backwards, and stalled. I was devastated. My face turned red. I wondered who was watching. My dad and uncle made it look so easy.

"I will drive this truck," I said out loud.

Once more I started the truck and this time I seemed more co-ordinated. Yes! The truck was moving backwards, but now I had to watch where I was going. Steering in those days was not easy. You really had to use both hands. Picture it. Two feet to manipulate three pedals, two hands to move the steering wheel, and one head to look backwards to see where you were headed. Luckily, the laneway between our house and the store was wide enough to manoeuver the vehicle without hitting anything.

I practised this routine each day because I wanted to be good enough for Dad to take me out in his black Ford car. The time came when I was nearly fourteen. It was a Wednesday afternoon. That was the only weekday when the store and the post office were closed. Dad drove me out to some country roads just outside of the hamlet of Golden Lake. And he let me drive the car. He guided me on the rules of the road: toot your horn when rounding a sharp corner, and always drive well over to your right when approaching the crest of a hill. I was in seventh heaven! My mother was very proud of me because when I became sixteen, I could get my driver's licence and take her shopping. Then she wouldn't have to feel that Dad was always waiting for her.

After that initial trip, my uncle let me drive his car with the rumble-seat, and took me out often to sharpen my driving skills. By the time I was fifteen, I would drive anyone's car if they let me. We teenagers would hang out at Dan Risto's lunch counter, and if any of the lads had a car, we would all pile in and go for a drive out on the country roads, or go to a movie in Eganville. Of course, I was still not old enough to drive on the highway, but I couldn't wait.

I turned sixteen in 1953, and guess what? There were cars now that had automatic transmissions and power steering. An older friend of mine who was already working bought one of these fine vehicles. He let me drive it on the highway! What a difference in getting started again when

Golden Lake train station, circa 1925. Standing in front are the four Knuth sisters: Annetta (Mrs. Jack Turner), Hattie (Mrs. Edgar Brant), Ida (Mrs. Reinhold Brose), and Gertrude (Mrs. Robert Brose).
Photo courtesy of Elaine Mundt.

you stopped at the stop sign. No more jerking! He even let me use his car to take the road test in Killaloe. I passed. I paid the five dollars for my licence and I was on the road.

It was much easier then—no need to take a written test and pay MONEY, no need for a sixty-day or a three-sixty-five licence and pay MONEY, and then the big road test and pay more MONEY. Just family and friends helping one another—teaching, guiding, and all the while having fun. But then there wasn't the amount of traffic on the roads as there is today. I believe, though, that my life as a driver, from its humble beginning, has made me a cautious, defensive, and patient operator of a motor vehicle. I have driven across Canada, on every kind of highway, in all kinds of weather, and feel so thankful that my dream of driving a car has become a wonderful reality.

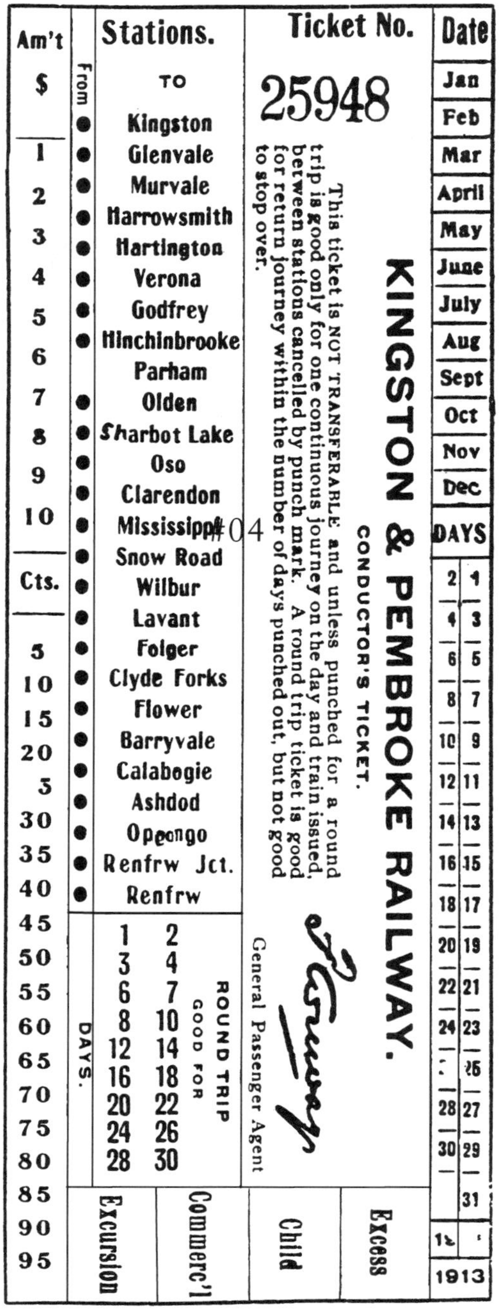

Am't $ 1 2 3 4 5 6 7 8 9 10 Cts. 5 10 15 20 25 30 35 40 45 50 55 60 65 70 75 80 85 90 95

Stations. From TO Kingston Glenvale Murvale Harrowsmith Hartington Verona Godfrey Hinchinbrooke Parham Olden Sharbot Lake Oso Clarendon Mississippi Snow Road Wilbur Lavant Folger Clyde Forks Flower Barryvale Calabogie Ashdod Opeongo Renfrw Jct. Renfrw

Ticket No. 25948

KINGSTON & PEMBROKE RAILWAY.

CONDUCTOR'S TICKET.

This ticket is NOT TRANSFERABLE and unless punched for a round trip is good only for one continuous journey on the day and train issued, between stations cancelled by punch mark. A round trip ticket is good for return journey within the number of days punched out, but not good to stop over.

General Passenger Agent

DAYS. ROUND TRIP GOOD FOR 1 2 3 4 6 7 8 10 12 14 16 18 20 22 24 26 28 30

Excursion Commerc'l Child Excess

Date Jan Feb Mar April May June July Aug Sept Oct Nov Dec DAYS 1–31 1913

Kingston & Pembroke Railway Ticket

Kingston & Pembroke Railway Ticket. The "Kick and Push," as it was affectionately known, transported passengers and freight between Kingston and Renfrew for the latter years of the nineteenth and much of the twentieth centuries. Construction began in 1872 but, after twelve years, had only reached as far as Renfrew—a distance of 112 miles. Lack of capital, difficult terrain, and competing lines meant that the railway never did reach its original destination of Pembroke. However, it did prove a popular means of connecting the many remote and isolated communities along its line. Today, the rails are gone from the K&P, but sections of the right-of-way have been preserved as recreation trails.

DO YOU MIND THE TIME . . .

My Little Grey House

by Dorothy (DeLaurier) Miller

My little grey house was built along the Madawaska River, we think, by the Isaac Duff family in the early nineteenth century. When I lived there, it was quite often referred to as the Duff Place. It was next to the place first owned by Donald McNaughton, on the east half of Lots 12 & 13, Concession 2. There were a total of 400 or 500 acres in all. The Stewart family purchased it in 1904 (or 1906) from the Duffs. My grandparents lived in this house until moving to the homestead in 1926. In the fall of 1933, my parents moved in and we all stayed until the spring of 1953.

The house was built with logs and later covered over by clapboards, which weathered into a shade of grey. The house still exists today, being used as a summer cottage. This is now a very old house. When we lived in it, it was thought to be about 140 years old.

My house never had electricity or running water, but growing up at the time when we did, this was not unusual. Later on we did get a telephone installed, I suspect, by my father. This indeed opened our lives up by quite a bit, mostly in our early teen years.

My house had seven rooms in it: three downstairs and four upstairs. There were two doors: the front door opened into the summer kitchen and the back door into the woodshed. Two stoves heated our home: a range in the kitchen and a box stove in the living room. There was also a range for use in the summer, which kept the rest of the house cooler. The kitchen ran the width of the house, and the living room and a spare bedroom took up the other half. At the top of the stairs stood one of the two closets. Down a hallway was the storage room and play room. Duncan and Earl, my brothers, shared one bedroom. My sister Irene and I shared another bedroom. It wasn't very big, but we did learn to share the space and duck our heads as it had one of the sloping ceilings. Plus, our room contained the other closet. It was a large walk-in closet, so that part was just fine with two growing girls.

For years we didn't pay any rent, but we did pay in other ways. We cut our wood from Grandpa's bush lot and brought it home by horse and

Irene and Dorothy DeLaurier at the back of the Little Grey House.

sleigh. We drew our water from a spring, which had the nicest water you could have. It was a fairly long piece to walk to! When we were still little, we used to carry water in a honey pail. Later, getting big enough, we used a big water pail. In the winter, it could get good and icy around the spring and you had to be careful or you would fall.

The boys used to feed the sheep, but Irene and I had the water to bring and also the wood, enough to fill the wood box. In the winter, we kept a large barrel in the house and we used it for laundry, bathing, and such things. This was kept filled with ice and snow that eventually melted.

In the winter, our outdoor play was skiing on the hills near the house. We also skated and used our sleighs a lot. It was nice when there was a nice crust on top of the snow, then sliding was good! Otherwise, we went over to the hill at Uncle Donald's and slid on it. That was a lot of fun.

In the summer, we played a lot around the creek that flowed all year round. We played house and sometimes, after a big storm, we would see if we could get the bridge to float away. This also happened in the spring. We had a wonderful barn to play in and, when filled with hay, we could hide in it. What wonderful summers we had! Irene and I picked wild strawberries, then raspberries, then blueberries. (Father didn't let us pick many blackberries because of the thorns.) All of this for winter desserts.

Our little grey house was not visible from the main road. You had to walk at least a half-mile to get out. This was a very private place to live and grow up. We had so many things to do that we were never bored.

Mother always kept our home clean. Our meals were simple, but filled us up. We were never hungry. We had a garden to grow our vegetables in. Irene and I used to make a smudge fire in an iron pot and carry it up and down the rows to keep mosquitoes away while Mother and Dad planted the garden. Irene and I also took the cows up to Grandpa's, where we got our milk, eggs, and butter. This worked well until one day the bull didn't want to go anywhere. I had a very scary time while he bawled and pawed the ground. Finally he walked away.

We got our first car in 1941—a 1929 Whippet touring car—which my father bought for $80 and kept repaired himself most of the time. Many drives and picnics were enjoyed on a summer Sunday. Father worked hard, but always took us to town to shop, go to the movies, etc. You could take the side curtains off the car for the summer and then snap them on in winter. The roof could fold back as well, but we didn't do that very often because it wasn't in very good shape.

Walking was something we did all the time. We had a two-and-a-half-mile walk to school and then the same home again. In summer we would walk up to Grandpa's and Arthur would take us swimming at Burnstown. We had over 500 acres to walk around, and we always felt perfectly safe. One of my favourite spots was a knoll with a maple tree on it. There I would daydream of my Prince Charming, who would come and sweep me off my feet! Well, my daydreams didn't all come true, but it was still a wonderful way to grow up.

Part of me will remain there, at the Little Grey House, forever. I know I can never walk down the hill, across the creek, and then up the little hill to that little grey house. Although I can't walk in to the smell of Mother's supper cooking, I can remember bringing in our wood and water for the night, doing homework and then having some time for myself.

Now, when I daydream, it is about the good times we shared growing up and living so close to my grandparents and friends. I am glad I had a little grey house and a sister who was and still is my best friend.

Mail Service

by Dolly Lenara McDonald

Most of my childhood has "mail memories" because my father serviced a rural mail route in the Northcote area for many years. So, before school registration and after summer holidays arrived, I'd accompany him on his daily route.

In all weather, we went from farm to farm, mail boxes on both sides of the road, and we delivered folks' mail, picked up the mail they wanted to send, and the paper-wrapped lumps of coins so as to buy the stamps "in town." When we got back to the Renfrew P.O., we would lick them and put them on for the farm folk and not mind it a bit!

In the summer we'd clean birds' nests out of the mailboxes after the eggs had hatched. Many were makeshift tin boxes, not "regulated" rural boxes like today. In the winter we'd clean the snow and ice out, so we could place the mail into the boxes tidily.

Cars had chains then, not snow tires, and many's the day my father had to crawl under the wheels to retrieve, repair, and replace chains that snapped from time to time. "All part of the job," he'd say, and struggle through it.

There were lots of rural mailmen like my father. No Purolator or Federal Express or private delivery then. Catalogues, parcels and packages were all hauled by the mail man and pleasantly and patiently so.

Life on the Farm

by Stella (Pershick) McMahon

Nicholaus Pershick, his wife Mary Ann (Kneba) Pershick and their two oldest sons, Ignatius and Anthony, came to Canada on a ship called *The Elba* in 1861. They came from Pomerania, the northern part of Poland. The people there were called Kashubs.

They lived in Renfrew at the time of the 1861 Census, but later moved to Admaston, Ontario, where they bought land and took up farming. The next four children—John, August, Mary and Margaret—were born here.

August inherited the farm and lived there with his wife, Margaret Switzer, and their twelve children. Eleven of them made it to adulthood. All are now deceased as of 2001, except for myself, the second youngest. Nicholaus and Mary Ann lived nearby in their own little home until their deaths. My mother, Margaret, passed away in 1948, and my father, August, in 1953. I turned eighty-seven in September 2001.

In the early years of my family's life on the farm, 1900 through the 1940s, the work was difficult. We lived mostly off the land. We raised cattle—cows for milk and butter; steers for the beef and the income in the fall; pigs for pork; fowl, including turkeys, for eggs and meat; sheep for wool as well as meat, and the income in the fall. We kept horses for help with the heavy work and for transportation. We planted and harvested grains, potatoes, hay, and we always had a large garden. We picked the wild strawberries, raspberries, blueberries, even blackberries, each in their own season, and we nurtured our apple trees for a healthy annual yield. The men cut, drew home, sawed, and chopped wood for our fuel, and we tapped the maple trees for making the maple syrup.

Stella (Pershick) McMahon on her eighty-sixth birthday, September 20, 2000.

The children attended school in a rural, one-room school house. One teacher juggled twenty or more pupils from Grade 1 to the high school levels. We had to walk about a mile-and-a-half to and from school. When it was stormy in winter, Dad would take us on the wood sleigh before he went to work in the bush. Sometimes a neighbour might bring us home, but most often we walked.

After school we had chores to do. Wood had to be brought in to fill the wood box for the night. Water had to be carried in for drinking, cooking, washing and bathing. When water was scarce, we would put a large barrel in a corner of the kitchen and carry in snow to melt for washing. When the chores were finished, and if we had a little time, we would take the toboggans and sleds out for a slide. We had some good hills and it was fun. Sunday afternoons were also spent sliding, or we would clear the snow from the pond behind the barn and go skating.

We had some bad times as well as the good. On one occasion the horses got scared and "ran away" from my brother. However, he held on to the reins and finally got them to stop about a half-mile away. He was shook up but otherwise okay. Another time two of my brothers were bringing in the ice to our icehouse where the blocks of ice were packed all around with a thick layer of sawdust. Insulated in this way the ice would stay frozen for the entire year's use. When my brothers, Michael and Bernard, went to the lake to get the ice blocks that had been cut earlier, Bernard slipped into the hole and nearly drowned. Michael got a board and put it across the hole. He pulled his brother out of the frigid water, and took him to a neighbour's fishing hut. There he made a fire and dried out Bernard's clothing. It was quite an ordeal for both of them. Needless to say, all the family at home had begun to worry when they were late getting home.

Some years, in the late fall and winter, water would be scarce and we had to take the cattle to the creek or the spring about a half-mile away, or herd them a mile-and-a-half down to the lake at the back of our property. Holes were cut in the ice for the cattle to drink. There was a road of sorts as pulpwood was hauled to Shanahan's Siding of the old K&P Railway. The pulpwood was piled in rows until there was enough. Boxcars would then be ordered from "the Railroad." The men would take lunches and load up the boxcars with the pulpwood. From there it was railed to the pulp mills.

Each year between Christmas and the New Year, the men would butcher a young steer. They would remove the head, hooves, and hide, and hang the carcass with the hay-fork-rope in the barn. After a couple of days they would quarter it and pack it in the milk house, a stone building that would keep the meat cool. I remember when I was in my teens my mother giving me the dish pan and a large butcher knife and asking me to climb up in the mow, where there was a plank stretched between the mows next to the carcass. I was instructed to cut off large steaks. My mother would hammer the steak to tenderize it, season it, flour it, and place it in a large iron fry pan with lots of onions. She would let it simmer to cook slowly at the back of the wood range. You don't get beef like that anymore.

During the winter, horses and sleighs were our means of transportation. My dad had a "cutter" and a double sleigh. On Sundays we got up early before the sun, put bricks in the oven to heat up, wrapped them in potato sacks and put them at our feet in the sleigh to keep warm on our way to church. We used a buffalo robe to cover our legs and knees.

Mother's sewing machine was always humming away, as she made patches for the quilt she was constructing. After she sewed the patches together into a large beautiful design, she placed the pattern onto a backing and fleece filling, and quilted it on a large frame. This tedious activity seemed a genuine pleasure for her. She hummed as she worked. When the quilt was finished we would all admire her masterpiece.

Dances and parties were always held at home. When I was about eight years old my mother and father celebrated their twenty-fifth wedding

Getting ready for a sleigh ride. 1920s.
Photo courtesy of Stella (Pershick) McMahon.

April brought the sawmill to the farm.
Photo courtesy of Stella (Pershick) McMahon.

anniversary. It was in January. Friends, neighbours, and relatives came to our home by horse and sleigh. My dad made room in the barns and stables to keep the horses out of the cold. He covered the horses with heavy blankets to help keep them warm. Several neighbour lads played the violin for dancing. We moved the table and chairs to the side of the large kitchen and placed two chairs on top of the table for the fiddlers. There was always a talented "caller" for the square dancing. One of our neighbours drank a little too much and wanted to step dance on the table. When they tried to discourage him, he grabbed a bottle and hit the wall, breaking the plaster. My dad was angry. That unfortunate incident spoiled the rest of the evening. In those days of Prohibition, some of the men made their own alcohol from grain in a big steel tub. They called it "hooch." It was very powerful.

The neighbours would also gather at someone's home for other social occasions in the winter. They played a card game called "forty-five." I never learned to play it, but we did play six- or four-hand euchre. I could play cards when I was about six years old.

Eventually the cold north winds and icy storms gave way to the sun and warmer temperatures of spring. Birds returned, built their nests and hatched a new brood, just as our barnyard fowl did. Of course, we kept a rooster and hens. The chicks were a favourite miracle of the springtime. We also raised turkeys that had to be carefully tended. The turkey hen never hatched her own eggs as our hens did. They would make nests in any long grass or mossy swamp. We would have to pen them up for a few hours, then let them loose and follow them to find their nests. When we had gathered enough—ten or twelve eggs—they were placed under a setting hen and she would hatch the turkey chicks just as if they were her own. Chicken eggs hatched in three weeks, but turkey eggs took four weeks. We also had to attend to the newborn spring lambs, calves, piglets and foals.

In spring, the wool would be clipped from the sheep and rolled up in fleeces. The sheep were predominately white, but now and again we would get a black one. The very best fleeces were saved for home use and the rest were sold. We would wash the wool and lay it out on the grass to dry. My mother would do what they called carding. Two boards with little picks in them were used to pull up the wool. Then she would spin it on her spinning wheel. Sometimes she would dye some of it for sweaters and socks. I can still see my mother knitting sweaters, socks and mittens for the family.

In late March the maple trees were tapped. Gathering the sap was hard work. Heavy pails of sap were emptied into cream cans or barrels on a horse-drawn sloop. They were taken and emptied into large pans to be boiled down over an open fireplace in the bush. Later the condensed sap was taken to the house, strained and further boiled down on the stove in large pots. Milk and beaten eggs were added to clear the syrup. Boiling was continued until the perfect consistency was achieved. It was strained again through cheesecloth. The maple syrup was then bottled for use during the following year.

April brought the sawmill to our farm to cut up that pile of "poles" in the yard that had been hauled home during the past winter. There was always a neighbour who had a sawmill. All the neighbours would come to help at our house and our men would go when they sawed theirs. It was all very neighbourly—almost a social event.

The planting was a busy season. Some ploughing had been done in the previous autumn, but most of it was done in the spring. Then the fields would be harrowed and cultivated before the grains were sown. I can still see my dad sowing grain by hand, carrying the pail on his arm. In later years it was done with a seed drill. Our garden was also planted in late May, and it was always a large one. My mother would start her tomato and cabbage seeds early in the house. Later we made a hot-house. A frame was made and placed over heated manure. Four storm windows were placed on top. It was quite efficient; we raised our own seedlings and even had early leaf lettuce. We always planted a large crop of potatoes. My dad would rotate the fields for a better yield. The seed was saved from the fall before. Occasionally a few bags of a new strain were bought. The field was ploughed in furrows with the horses. The children walked behind the plough dropping the seed potatoes in neat rows. Then they were covered up with another pass of the plough. During the summer the potato field had to be cultivated between the rows. The corn was planted in the same way.

In the spring we would pick dandelions and my mother would make wine. Raspberries, blackberries, black cherries, and butternuts also made good wine. Among Mother's many talents was soap-making. She used rendered lard and added lye. She boiled it outside on a clear day in a large pot over a fireplace. She whipped it and let it cool some before she shaped it into cakes. Mother's soap sudsed well in the soft water from the rain barrel. The soap was applied directly to the clothes and they were scrubbed on a washboard in big wooden tubs.

Besides cultivating and weeding the garden, potato and corn fields, the summer months were spent cutting, raking, stooking, and bringing in the hay with the horse-drawn wagon which was always overloaded. One of my brothers manoeuvred the team and the wagon to just below the door to the hay mow. A large hay fork operated with rope and pulleys lifted huge mounds of hay into the mow where it was forked evenly about the mow for storage and use during the late fall, winter and spring to feed the cattle and horses.

Harvesting wheat. The threshing machine was taken from farm to farm.

Photo courtesy of Stella (Pershick) McMahon.

Berry-picking was getting out into the fields and picking wild strawberries. We had our favourite places to pick. One was called the "Brushes." It was on the side of a hill with lots of sumacs and small trees—ideal for berry-picking. Raspberries were found mostly along the stone fences and stone piles at the edges of the fields. There were often blackberries to be found also. For blueberries, we had to go farther afield, as they didn't grow on our farm. Berries were wonderful served fresh with cream, and mother always made plenty of jam for the winter months.

In the fall, there would always be a teachers' convention. The children, being home from school for two or three days, would dig and bag the potatoes. They would be stored in large bins in the root cellar.

The highlight of the fall was the threshing of the harvested oats and wheat. The threshing machine was taken from farm to farm and it was always a big event. Run by a wood-fired engine, the machine used a system of belts. The grains were separated and bagged, and the straw was blown into barn mows and the cow shed loft. The women would prepare for a couple of days, baking pies and cakes, and preparing vegetables and meat. There would be ten or more men helping; a feast was prepared. After the fields were cleared of crops the cattle were put there to pasture.

At one time my father would take grain to the Douglas gristmill and have it ground into flour. I can remember the wooden breadbox in the corner of the kitchen, and later a round tin bread pan the size of a small tub was used. We baked bread three or four times a week. We used fairy yeast; there was always a jar of starter on the window and then potato water was added. Later we used cakes of yeast and eventually it was available in packages.

We would gather in the kitchen in the fall to cut up cabbage and mother would make a barrel of sauerkraut. Carrots, turnips and parsnips were all prepared and stored in sand in a bin in the cellar. We always had our own supply of apples stored in a cool part of the cellar. From our large McIntosh tree we had hand-picked the apples, wrapped them in newspaper, and placed them in hampers for storage. The Northern Spy provided apples that we stored in the same way for baking pies, apple upside-down-cake, applesauce and cider.

Early in the fall, the men would butcher a pig; mother would make the head cheese and blood sausage. No part of the animal was wasted. The turkeys had to be fattened for Thanksgiving and Christmas feasts. The sheep were sold in the fall; we kept only a few to breed over the winter.
We always milked ten or twelve cows, separated the milk, and saved the cream. We kept some of the whole milk for drinking and a little cream for table use, but the remaining skimmed milk

was used with mash to feed the pigs. We kept the cream cool in the cellar until it was almost sour. With a hand-operated Daisy churn we worked the cream up and down with a paddle until the butter formed. The remaining milk was called buttermilk. My mother had a large round wooden tub in which the butter was placed. Then we would carry cold water from the spring well—all up hill—to wash the remaining buttermilk out of the butter that hardened when the cold water washed over it. A bit of salt and some butter colour was added in the winter. We called it dairy butter. Sometimes the cows went dry in winter so my mother made sure we had enough butter stored in crocks for that period.

In the early 1930s, my mother became ill. She suffered from diabetes. Insulin had just been discovered and she was treated with needles three times a day. She couldn't administer it herself so the girls at home all learned how. The doctor in Ottawa predicted she would live for only five years, but she survived for almost fifteen. She did her own testing two or three times a week with a Bunsen burner and had to watch her diet very carefully. I had been to high school at Mount St. Patrick, but at Grade 10 I had to quit to stay home and look after Mother. I stayed with her until I was married on November 6, 1940, by which time my brother was running the farm and was prosperous enough to have a tractor and a truck.

A Day in December

by Wes Bomhower

December 27, 1924, dawned crisp and clear along the Madawaska River. Snow had fallen the past two days and it sparkled now in the early morning sunlight. Up in the loft of the big log house the younger children were stirring as the sweet aroma of buckwheat pancakes and maple syrup wafted through the open trap door. Big John Stubinsky had already left for work a mile or so upstream where he manned the powerhouse that supplied power to the Black Donald Graphite Mines.

Beatrice, who like her parents had a bedroom on the ground floor, was the oldest girl at home and the third eldest of eight children. An older sister, Agnes, had married the previous year. Mrs. Stubinsky was more than seven months pregnant and today meant another day of hard work for Beatrice. No school until next week so there was water to haul for the wash, bread to bake and other day-to-day household chores. Beatrice didn't mind though. It was a break from the daily trek to and from the one-room school five miles away beyond Black Donald Village. The existing roads were mere bush trails and often after a snowfall the children had to flounder through deep drifts to reach their destination. Teachers were very unforgiving to pupils who showed up after the nine o'clock bell.

There were few neighbours, but the Stubinskys were self-sufficient, Beatrice mused as she cleaned up the breakfast table. There were chickens, pigs, a few cows, a team of horses, and a pony in the little log barn and vegetables in the root cellar from last summer's garden. She had helped her mother "do up" numerous jars of wild berries, which grew in abundance on the hillside by the river, and a good supply of maple syrup remained from last spring's sugar season.

Her thoughts drifted back to last spring and the break-up of ice on the Madawaska River. For some reason she could not explain, the wild swirling waters and huge ice floes fascinated her to no end. The ice would build up to a certain point then with a roar everything was released in a maelstrom of spraying water and broken ice. She almost felt she was part of the river. She wondered if other people felt it, too, and considered asking her mother. But no, she would wait. Perhaps it's just my age, she reasoned. I'm not a child, but not quite a woman. She remembered the appraising stares of the bearded "shantymen" and river drivers as they portaged past on the log drives later in the spring, and it made her conscious of her changing body. She made a mental note to ask her mother a lot of questions after the baby was born; sometime when the younger children were not around.

She kneaded the dough for a batch of fresh bread and got it ready for the oven of the big wood range. Beatrice's older brother, Albert, whooped and waved as he passed the window driving the team and sleigh on some errand and Mrs. Stubinsky retired to the bedroom. Beatrice hummed a lively Irish tune she remembered from last Saturday night at the Black Donald Community Hall. She had turned fifteen and her parents had allowed her to accompany Albert to the annual Christmas dance. Oh, the sound of the fiddles still rang in her ears and that handsome boy from Mount St. Patrick had kept her on the dance floor for every square dance.

She was re-living the wonderful evening when an anguished cry from her mother interrupted her reverie. Rushing into her parents' bedroom, she found her mother gasping in pain beside the bed. "Get Dad and the doctor," Mrs. Stubinsky managed between stifled cries. Beatrice needed no prompting and raced to the telephone. She tried to call her father first at the powerhouse, but could get no dial tone, and in desperation almost shook the old telephone set off the wall. Calm down, she told herself, and picked up the receiver again to call the doctor in Calabogie. All she heard was a series of clicks and squawks. "Damn telephone, never does work when you need it," she muttered, then immediately crossed herself for swearing.

In a quiet voice she gave orders to her younger sister and called out to her mother, "Hang on Mom, I'll get help right away." Feeling not nearly as confident as she sounded, Beatrice grabbed her coat and boots and ran for the little log barn. She quickly saddled the pony, the only mode of transportation at her disposal, and flew down the trail toward the mine some three miles distant. The phone always works well there, she reasoned, even better than at the powerhouse.

They approached a small bridge and the pony balked and refused to cross, finally bolting back up the trail toward home. Beatrice managed to get the pony stopped, yanked the saddle off and cried, "Go you crazy so-and-so," as the pony galloped up the homeward trail. With tears of frustration streaming down her cheeks, she struggled through the deep snow toward the mine again.

With every step she prayed for strength and courage, and especially for her mother. Beatrice was no stranger to childbirth (all her siblings had been born at home), but instinctively she knew this pregnancy was different. The baby was not due for at least six weeks. Mrs. Stubinsky never complained, but Beatrice had sensed a difference in her mother lately.

She reached the mine office and staggered breathlessly through the door. The surprised clerk listened to her story and was on the phone instantly to John Stubinsky at the powerhouse. Next he called the doctor in Calabogie with instructions to make haste to the Stubinsky homestead.

A neighbour stopped by as Beatrice warmed herself by the mine office's pot-bellied stove and offered her a horse to drive home. A nurse who was visiting the neighbour came along to help.

Big John Stubinsky was at his wife's bedside when Beatrice and the nurse returned. He reluctantly left the bedroom at the nurse's request. Through all their married years he had never seen his wife so weak and deathly pale. He sat in the old rocker and poured out his feelings to Beatrice, the daughter who was so like her mother: quiet and reserved, but strong when the need arose. Tears welled in his big brown eyes and trickled through a stubble of beard on his weatherbeaten face. Beatrice had never seen this big man cry before and she knew she must comfort him if even to hide her own feelings. "Oh Dad," she soothed, "everything will be all right when the doctor gets here." But she had a terrible foreboding that nothing would ever be the same again.

The doctor made the best time he could with horse and sleigh, and arrived about four in the afternoon, but to no avail. Mrs. Stubinsky died shortly after his arrival. The doctor estimated the baby had been dead for two weeks and the deadly poison from the fetus had killed the mother. She was only thirty-seven years of age.

With a heavy heart Beatrice assumed her mother's responsibilities and raised the family. She later married and raised a family of her own. Although the big log house, the powerhouse, the village of Black Donald, and the Black Donald Graphite Mines no longer exist (all were flooded when Ontario Hydro built the Mount Chute dam), Beatrice still lives nearby in her own home overlooking Black Donald Lake. Above a huge fieldstone fireplace hangs a beautiful picture of Annie (Hisko) Stubinsky, Beatrice's mother, a poignant reminder of another time and a certain day in December.

> ***"Add five to ten per cent to greases, one to five per cent to oils, or one teaspoonful per pint of oil. The SPECIAL FUNCTION of graphite is to even up the minute irregularities found in all bearing surfaces. BLACK DONALD FLAKE GRAPHITE is the purest, toughest graphite on the Canadian market and is specially fitted by nature for this particular purpose."***
>
> **— Directions on the back side of a yellow tin of No. 2 Fine Flake Black Donald graphite. A highland piper graced the front. The Black Donald Mine (1896–1954), twenty kilometres west of Calabogie, produced the only high-quality graphite suitable for lubricants in North America.**

Shanties

by Garry Ferguson

> *Come all you jolly lumberjacks*
> *And listen to my song.*
> *It's all about the shanty boys*
> *And how they get along.*
>
> – Old Folk Song

The term logging shanty not only brings to mind a specific period in our history, but it denotes a way of life. The hard life of the shantyman spawned a pride, an attitude, a culture rich in song and legend. The Bunyan (Bunion) tales were lifted from this culture by U.S. writers.

The shanties in my part of the country, Renfrew County, were usually one-room log hovels with dirt floors. The builders used moss to chink the cracks and overlapped scooped logs to fashion a roof.

In the centre of the room sat a rectangular platform of earth and sand cribbed up with logs. A fire for cooking, heat and light burned on this camboose twenty-four hours a day. Over the camboose a wooden vent protruded through the roof. Though designed as a flu, this opening probably served as a health feature as well as releasing more than smoke from a room filled with men who went to sleep with bellies full of baked beans. One of my grandfathers, who worked in the shanties, said that when the vent ignited, as it often did, it was every man outside to heave snow at the fire.

The straw-covered, two-man bunks made of poles were used for more than just a bed. The men virtually lived on them. At mealtime they would heap their plates with beans and salted beef or pork, fill their shanty tins with tea or soup, grab a chunk of pot-baked bread, and head back to their bunks. Here they did a balancing act while they "shoved 'er back" with a spoon and a knife. I wondered why the same grandfather used a knife to put food to his mouth instead of a fork until I learned that the shantyman was provided with a spoon only. He provided his own all-purpose knife which he learned to use with dexterity when it came to "shovelling grub."

When it came time to "hit the hay," the men peeled off down to their ganzies (underwear), often turning them inside out to foil the lice until they could get to sleep. Sometime during the night, after the little vermin had cuddled up to them again, they'd get up, turn the underwear right-side-out and go back to sleep. The only baths were suffered by those unlucky enough to fall through the ice of some lake or stream.

For six days a week, all hands would be up at four in the morning. Horses and men had to be fed so that the crews would be on the job at daylight. Logs were cut, skidded, and hauled to waterways to catch spring floods that would carry them to ships bound for markets in Britain. They knew it was quitting time when the sun went down.

By the time my father went to the bush, tar-papered camps with stoves, plank tables, and ticks on the bunks had replaced the shanty. Life was easier because the mechanized age meant that men were no longer as isolated, but the folklore of the shanties still survived. The legends, songs, work ethic, and skills had all been inherited from the shantymen.

The mentality of men who "went to shanty" and the women who stayed behind to run homesteads and raise families was forged in the hardships of an unforgiving time in an unforgiving land. They took pride in self-sufficiency, mental and physical toughness. It's not unusual to hear older folk talk of past privations with such pride that you might believe they'd do it all over again. Their values and traits became so entrenched in society that they are still an inherent part of the Canadian identity.

"Before the Ottawa, Arnprior & Parry Sound Railway was built through the lumber country [1890s], large quantities of shanty supplies of all kinds were gathered at Arnprior and forwarded from there by teams of the firm's shanties on the Madawaska and Bonnèchere. For instance, in the heyday of lumbering, McLachlin Brothers' pork order every year was 1,000 barrels of Chicago heavy mess, which used to arrive in November or December in one shipment of 10 carloads. There were also carloads of beans, flour, sugar, syrup and numerous other groceries. The yearly purchases of hay ran into hundreds of tons and of oats into thousands of bushels; but these commodities were mostly bought from settlers near the shanties who delivered the goods direct themselves.

"The first shanty gangs were sent up in early September. Many men were hired around Arnprior and a fine lot of workers came from the surrounding country, from White Lake, Burnstown, Springtown, Calabogie, Renfrew and Eganville. Mount St. Patrick was noted for its tall Irishmen, all excellent shantymen. But the bulk of the hiring was done in Ottawa which, even when it was as Bytown, was the chief gathering place for shantymen from all over the country. Many came from the Province of Quebec, a considerable number from as far away as Gaspé, where they were fishermen in summer and worked in the shanties in winter."

— Charles Macnamara, McLaughlin Brothers Lumber Company, circa 1885.
During the 1880s—the glory days of the lumbering trade—the following companies worked limits in the Madawaska drainage basin: McLachlin Bros., Perley and Pattee, J.R. Booth, Bronson and Weston, William Mason, E.B. Eddy Mfg. Co. Ltd., and many others.

John and Elaine Gardam, August 27, 1955.

A Soldier's Memories of Renfrew County

by Colonel John Gardam (Ret.)

My training in Camp Borden had come to an end and I was told I had been commissioned in the Royal Canadian Dragoons based in Camp Petawawa, Ontario. I had hoped to go back to my former regiment, The Lord Strathconas Horse (Royal Canadians) in Calgary.

Three of us, all brand new second lieutenants, took the train to Petawawa in January 1952. As the train stopped in Pembroke the conductor said, "The whole town is on fire!" We could see a glow in the sky, but little else. Later we found out that Doran's Ladies Wear had burned down. That was my first glimpse of Renfrew County.

The regiment was a busy place. "C" Squadron was in Germany with 27 Brigade and a huge excess of soldiers were being recruited for the new NATO commitment. I was given command of a group of soldiers from Toronto quartered in the basement of Bessborough Hall.

The regiment was composed of three groups: those who fought in the Second World War, those who had just joined for NATO, and newcomers like myself. The commanding officer was John Merner who had recently married Laura Lacey from Pembroke.

As time went by I was put in charge of training wheeled vehicles drivers and, as such, spent hours driving the country roads in and about Renfrew County. Little did I realize that in 1967 I would buy a cottage on Wilson's Bay on the Bonnechere River, just off the Tramore Road near Deacon. Some thirty years later I wrote this story on our kitchen table at the same cottage.

In the early 1950s, I met Elaine Wood of Pembroke. We were married in Wesley United Church in Pembroke on August 27, 1955. Our first son, John, was born in the Cottage Hospital in Pembroke in October 1956. Our third son, David, was also born in the same hospital on December 24, 1959. Our second and fourth sons were born in Ottawa and Kingston.

As the years went by, I started to work with Ferret scout cars and saw many parades in the county—November 11th parades in Pembroke, recruiting parades in Arnprior and Renfrew. One

Colonel John Gardam while with the Fort Garry Horse.

cold winter day, my scout cars travelled the icy roads near Calabogie searching for a lost hunter. (He was never found.)

In 1958, I was rebadged to the Fort Garry Horse and a year later was on the farewell parade in Petawawa as the squadron left for a year in Egypt, our task being to patrol the desert between Arab and Israelis along the international frontier.

After my return from Egypt, I was sent to Ottawa where my wife Elaine and I now live. I will always remember my time in Petawawa and Pembroke with fond memories of the townspeople, the shopkeepers and, above all, the countryside. Renfrew County has a beauty and serenity, which in time of war and in peace has been a great place for soldiers to serve. Petawawa is one of the finest training areas in all of Canada.

During the Great Ice Storm of 1998, the soldiers went all over the county to bring a normal life back for the inhabitants. In time of forest fires they have been there to give aid when needed.

The bond between the people who have made Renfrew County their home has also given soldiers memories they will treasure for the rest of their lives.

Tobacco Farming in Renfrew County

by Guy Jamieson

When I tell people that as a teenager I spent my summer holidays picking tobacco, they naturally assume that I did so in southern Ontario. When I explain that it was on a farm just ten minutes from Renfrew, they look at me in disbelief.

The story of Renfrew County's tobacco farming began in 1957 when Horton Township's Andrew Johnston decided to grow a seven-acre experimental crop on the family's fifth concession homestead. With the assistance of the Department of Agriculture in Renfrew, and the financial backing of North Star Feeds, a greenhouse was constructed, seedlings were sown, and before long the first young tobacco plants were transplanted to the field. Through the rest of that summer these inaugural plants were carefully watered, cultivated, suckered, and topped, and in due time the first harvest was made.

The results of that harvest proved that the Horton fields aptly provided the appropriate light sandy soil required for the tobacco plants, and the experimental crop was deemed a great success. The next year a formal partnership was established between Andrew Johnston and North

Picking tobacco at Andrew Johnston's farm. (L–R) Glen Toner, Bob Johnston, Guy Jamieson, Burt Virgin, David Jamieson, Kent Smith.

Star Feeds, creating Johnston Tobacco Farms Limited. Dedicated to this new crop, the Johnston family increased their tobacco acreage to twenty-seven acres, and built a pack barn and several kilns. They hired a suite of employees consisting of a priming crew, tiers, leaf handlers, a tractor driver, a kiln hanger, and a cure man. Tobacco farming in Renfrew County had now begun in earnest.

The job of primers was given to local teenagers, and we would arrive daily in the field at 7:00 a.m., along with our horse that pulled the tobacco boats. Our gang consisted of five, and our daily routine saw us choosing our row, bending down beside the dew-soaked plants, and plucking the sand leaves next to the ground. You stayed bent until you had a good load under your arm, which you placed in the boat, then you returned to your row for more. After the sand leaves were all stripped from the plants, we moved up to seconds, then to thirds, fourths, and then to tips. What a relief it was for the back when we got to tips! You did this all day until the kiln was filled or your back gave out! (Later on we would easily appreciate Stompin' Tom when he sang, "Tillsonburg, my back still hurts when I hear that word.")

From the fields the leaves were hauled to the kiln area where they were unloaded onto a table. Leaf handlers placed the leaves into bundles of three, and handed them to a tier who tied them onto a slat. The slat looked like a four-foot snow fence, and it was sent up an elevator into the kiln where the kiln hanger placed them on rafters until the kiln was full. The gas heat was turned on and the kiln monitored for seven days. By then the leaves were flue-cured and ready to be taken to the pack barn. All of this exacting process was the sole responsibility of the cure man, who staffed the kilns twenty-four hours a day, seven days a week . The Johnston's cure man lived on site, and hailed from North Carolina. (Boy how we loved that "you-all" accent!)

The harvest lasted from mid-August until the end of September, when a big harvest party capped the season. By then we were happy to go back to high school, college or university, try to get caught up in our studies, or try to make the football team—after our friends had three weeks' head start. But we had our winter's spending money in the bank and a lot of fond memories of our summer activities. It was close to Christmas before the tobacco tar stains were gone from our arms and legs. No wonder so few of us took up smoking!

During the fall on the tobacco farm, tobacco graders were hired. The graders worked from October until Christmas, sorting through the cured tobacco. The graders would bale the tobacco and prepare it for delivery to Delhi, Ontario, which held the Dutch Auction process.

As 1958 drew to a close, the first full-production year at Johnston's Tobacco Farm successfully ended, and thoughts turned to a promising future.

In 1959, the tobacco crop on the Johnston farm was expanded to a total of forty-five acres. Our priming gang returned for another season, and over the next couple of years other gangs were assembled as three more tobacco farms sprung up in the neighbourhood. Bill Winters, Larry Kasaboski, and Charles Heffern of Beachburg all became fully engaged in the tobacco business. Each farm would keep the same priming gang each summer and, like the old-time logging crews, we had our friendly rivalries, such as competing to see who could fill a kiln the fastest.

As the 1960s wore on, the sun eventually set on Renfrew County's tobacco industry. By early 1965, due to poor health, Mr. Johnston retired from the tobacco industry and died in October of the same year. In the following years, Charlie Heffern was killed in a plane crash and, due to falling tobacco prices, threats of early frost, higher input costs, and smaller markets, Messrs. Winters and Kasaboski sold their tobacco rights and returned to more traditional farming. By the early 1970s, the flue-cured tobacco industry in Renfrew County had ended.

Like the shanty and railway days, our county's tobacco industry has become a historical footnote. But for those of us who were employed in the tobacco fields of Renfrew County, we still have many memories of our close-knit gangs that seemed to do everything together. As many of us approach our sixties, each of us reflects back on the hard, dirty work we endured six days a week. More importantly though, we smile and laugh at the good times we had, which well out-weighed the job we had to do. And although we are scattered all over the country today, when we do get together at weddings, funerals, anniversaries and homecomings, we always reminisce about the noon-hour touch football games, our softball teams, musical bands, drive-in movies, and girlfriends. And so we hope that as you pass by those former tobacco farms, you may spot a kiln or two standing as testimony to the hubbub of activity and the hustle and bustle of young people that once existed.

Yes my friend, there really were tobacco farms in Renfrew County!

Some members of the Horton priming gangs:

Johnston Gang
Guy Jamieson, Art Jamieson, David Jamieson, Bob Johnston, Kent Smith, Denzil Ferguson, Dick Rodgers, Burt Virgin, Charlie Kitts, Findlay Barr, Buster MacGregor, David George, Glen Toner.

Winters Gang
Butch Brown, Art Brown, Gary Eady, Ricky Livingstone, Gerry Livingston, Calvin McLaughlin, Basil MacMillan, Bobby Schwartz and Carl Rits.

Kasaboski Gang
Ronnie Kasaboski, Mike Chapeski, Gerard O'Shea

The Old Ice House

by R. Ernest Jukes

Remember those inky black nights, that unless we had a full moon overhead, we would have to stumble our way to and from the outhouse, usually successfully, but more by habit and luck than sight? It was a lucky fellow, too, that got a flashlight for Christmas, as batteries seemed a costly phenomena in those days. Many of us can still recall our grandparents, parents, and even ourselves using coal oil lamps for light—albeit a source for tired eyes, but still better than candles.

Fairly reliable wood stoves were used for heating, cooking, and producing hot water. A few people used kerosene stoves during the hot summer months and some folks even had a summer kitchen to reduce the heat of cooking. Do you mind those evenings when we listened to CBC and our favourite mystery and adventure programs, like the *Lone Ranger*, or *The Shadow* and certainly *Hockey Night in Canada*? The radios were powered by large batteries almost the size of the receiver, and meant eventually driving into Renfrew for replacements.

That was in the times when our highlands were B.H.—that is "before hydro." Yes, those were the good old days when we used underground cold caches, called root cellars, to keep our veggies and venison from spoiling. Of course, we sometimes had to go a step further to pickling, smoking and preserving our favourite game, fish and foods, like all those jams and fruits to be enjoyed later. These were not easy days, but all the hard work stood for personal quality, usually large quantity, and always so much flavour that somehow it seems difficult to duplicate those same tastes today.

As time rolled along we gradually evolved to bright naphtha "pumper" lights to read by, with "pumper" clothes washers, and even iceboxes to keep food safe and tasty. Just so long as we had that important commodity—ice. And of course in these here hills we didn't have ice delivery, but we had our own methods by pooling our manpower and resources. In the dense and frosty thick of winter when the lakes froze to that same frigid consistency and proper thickness, it was time to "haul up the ice."

Just about everyone had a frame or log ice house. It was usually situated in a shady area, although some were part of a barn or outbuilding. There was an opening to fill the blocks of ice from the top and a doorway to remove them with ice tongs from the bottom. The "iceman" was careful to replace insulating sawdust over the remaining tiers.

It was usually real nose drippin' weather when the ice was harvested in our neck of the woods. We never heard of anyone going through, but I am reminded of an old Inuit proverb that you don't know your friend from your enemy until the ice breaks. The ice in our local area was drilled and hand-sawn into blocks from Billy MacPherson's or Joe McLaren's Lakes and sledded out by a strong team of horses. They came up through Colin John Thompson's lane to be stacked into the ice houses along the way, then covered with sawdust previously hauled up Johnny Robert's Hill from Billy Thomson's sawmill on the Madawaska River. It would take many trips to supply most of the homes along the Frontenac and Settlement Roads at Matawatchan. The ice supply from these lakes would more than satisfy their refrigeration needs right through to the following year.

Those shanty roofs were usually covered with tarps and boards to protect the large stack of ice blocks from rain as well as the hot rays of the Madawaska Valley's spring and summer sun. It was quite a simple matter with an ice pick or hatchet to pry out a thirty-pound block of crystal clear ice from the neat, tight pile. There was the usual chipping off of a few pieces to suck on, more if a gang of lads were around. We would hook on the iron ice tongs to carry the chunk outside, rinse off the sawdust, and then carry it into the kitchen icebox. Mom was always ready to open and close the doors, and mop up the trail of water drips behind us.

The old ice house offered many other advantages, too. As a kid it was a "cool" place to get out of sight on a hot afternoon when someone was calling you for chores, and even on a rainy day for that matter if a young lad was really pressed. It was not an unpleasant spot at all; there was a dank, but nice woody smell about the place. As time went on and one grew older, it was also a perfect spot both to keep the beer cold and chill a bottle of wine or soda pop before heading out for the dance. Some ice houses doubled as a large, walk-in cold room when the icebox just couldn't handle the hanging game, beef, pork, or additional summer refreshments. It was also a simple, perhaps a masculine type of place to "hang out" with cronies and sip on something appropriate for a warm summer's day.

At special times we would go out to the ice house and chip a pile of ice pieces. They would be placed, along with cream and the appropriate amounts of sugar, vanilla and coarse salt, into a wooden bucket apparatus called an ice cream maker. There was never a lack of enthusiastic young volunteers who would religiously crank the device, soon turning out the smoothest, most delicious Sunday afternoon treat. We still have it at Camp J and it still works just as well with ice cubes today. It seems we Canucks have always been adept at what we do with and on the ice.

Well all good things seem to come to an end and this important part of our heritage, like so many other valuable and charming items of yesterday, disappeared with a simple flick of a switch. Stoves and fridges, pumps and plumbing, irons and showers, gas and oil furnaces all seemed to instantly flood into our valley, just as fast as Ontario Hydro could install the poles and lines. It was 1954, and electricity had at last arrived in our little pocket of the province, one of the last areas of Ontario, in spite of us producing almost half of North America's electrical power—and the Madawaska providing the sixth largest generating facility!

Hydro-electricity quickly pushed the ice house into becoming a relic of the past and continued to lead us into an era of electronics we had never known.

However, in spite of the physical labour that went into our technology of yesterday, I believe many of you will agree with me that our early methods also included a lot of good clean fun. And haven't those simple times moulded a lot of fine people that affect our society in a positive way today? We also know that like the ice house and the electric refrigerator, change will continue to come to our Madawaska Highlands of Renfrew County and, we trust, improve our style of life in future years. Remember that man's greatest technology is still an idea.

Camp J Ice House. *Sketch by R.E. Jukes.*

HAVE YOU EVER BEEN TO . . .

This Cabin

by R. Ernest Jukes

There's an old cabin on a mountain top
Not so very far away,
The scent of pines beckon us there
To visit yesterday.

A place that remains unchanged
Offering constant peace of mind,
A special space to rekindle our spirits
While taking us back in time.

From this retreat, generations have wielded
Paddle, axe, rod and gun as well as brush
and pen,
Its environment inspires re-creation while
Leading us back to nature again.

The thick pine walls could tell us stories
Of life, death, laughter and tears,
Cheering those they sheltered from heat or chill
Throughout its hundreds of years.

The snowshoes hung, recall deep storms
When even horse and sleigh were stayed,
The homestead stove, oil lamps and quilts
Provided comfort to those that worked and
sometimes played.

An old log cabin on Carswell's Mountain
Is still waiting for us there,
To enjoy again its enduring pleasures
For all of us to share.

Dreams of Golden Lake

by Gail Mills

The quiet moon's image is reflected in ripples on beautiful Golden Lake. My windows are open on this warm summer night, and the breeze from the lake flutters my lace curtains. I can hear soothing sounds of trees swaying, a hundred frogs' nighttime chorus, and a whippoorwill singing in the distance. As the waves gently caress the shore, I find myself drifting off into a dream-filled sleep.

In these dreams, snapshots of my life on the shores of Golden Lake blend together in my mind's eye. My first vision is of me in my yellow paddleboat, and I am eagerly exploring the nooks and crannies of the shoreline. As a child, I was always pretending to be a detective, and on this sunny afternoon, I might find a clue. The sun warms me, and I head out to deeper waters, where I can fling my stone anchor into the cool depths and dive into the refreshing water.

This memory fades and another picture comes to life in my dreamland. My aunt, cousin, and I are floating in the tall reed patches on our water mattress built for three.

"Watch out for those alligators!" my aunt yells, and we small girls pound the sparkling waters with our legs to escape the imaginary reptiles. This game continues for hours, and we never seem to tire of it.

One of the dearest memories in my heart is the family barbecues that we would host in our backyard by the lake. I see these reunions in my slumber; we are hungrily eating hamburgers and macaroni salad, after splashing around in the lake for hours. We would then sit outside, watching the sun set across the lake, and go inside to continue our conversation and a game of cards—only after the mosquitoes and blackflies chased us there.

Visions of summer dissolve into scenes of winter on Golden Lake. I see myself twirling and sliding on our private backyard skating rink, with Elizabeth Manley and Katarina Witt coaching me on.

I can picture the time that Mom and I zoomed across the wind-swept ice. The snowless lake was a giant rink, and we ventured on our skates as far as Big Island.

Now, I am on the back of our "Motoski," clinging to Dad as we plunge through snowdrifts on our way to the fish-house. We sit, waiting and watching patiently, listening to the crackle of the wood stove between us. A fish comes into view through the hole, hovering at our bait for a moment, and continues on its way through the weedy depths.

I feel total peace and contentment as the next vista enters my mind. I am sitting on the soft lawn with my springer spaniel, Toby, at my side. The evening breeze blows tenderly across my face, and both the lake and sky shine blue and pink, with hues of purple in-between. The moon is rising in the east, and as I sit here, my eyes fill with tears. No matter where I go or who I become, I know that Golden Lake will always be a part of me.

The alarm startles my slumbering mind. My eyes open to sunshine and birds chirping their morning songs. Another day has begun on the shores of Golden Lake.

"The scenery of the Ottawa is not, perhaps, equalled, in point of grandeur, by any portion of the Canada, unless by that of the St. Lawrence. From Bytown to that part of the Ottawa known as the 'Deep River,' the Ottawa flows through a wide spreading valley, and has more the appearance of a succession of large lakes than that of a river. These lakes are generally studded with groups of islands, and add much to the beauty of the landscape ."

— David Thompson, explorer, who was engaged by the Commissioners, Survey of the Ottawa River, November–December 1837.

"It [the Ottawa River] is not so much a river in the English sense of the word, as a chain of lakes, or long sheets of quiet water, twenty, thirty and sixty miles in length each, connected by narrows and rapids, by which the river forces its way through high and rocky lands in a series of cascades and foaming currents."

— Dr. John J. Bigsby, May 1821, in his report on the geology of Upper Canada

The O'Grady Settlement, Hagarty Township

by Tom and Shirley Connolly

High in the hills of Hagarty Township, in the southern most part of the township close to the 16th Concession of Brudenell, there is a long and winding dirt road called O'Grady Settlement Road. There are no O'Gradys living on the road or in the area now, but once upon a time there were many—in fact, seven brothers and six sisters, and their spouses and families.

The first members of the family arrived in Hagarty Township in the late 1850s. On the 1861 Census for Nipissing District which then encompassed this area, three O'Grady brothers—John, Martin and Henry—were shown as residents in the yet unsurveyed township. The three young men were probably all living together because when the original survey map was registered in L'Original in August 1862 and returned for sale in October of the same year, it recorded the name of Thomas O'Grady on Lot 25 and his son Martin on Lot 24, Concession 1. Soon there were many O'Gradys in the area. Yet, almost a century-and-a-half later, only Martin's homestead is still owned by a descendant of the family and the significance of the road name is not widely known.

This, therefore, is the story of the long and winding road travelled by the O'Grady family, from the gently rolling fields of their Irish homeland to these bush lots in Renfrew County.

The O'Grady family came to Canada in 1826 from the Parish of Kilbarron, in the County of Tipperary. Coincidentally, this parish is part of the Diocese of Killaloe in Ireland. The patriarch of the family, John O'Grady, was a small farmer with a holding of five-and-three-quarter acres that he rented from a gentleman, Thomas Sadleir. He supplemented his income by working as a landlord's agent. In later years, his son James was quoted as saying:

> "Father wore top boots and leather breeches and rode about to fairs doing business for a Jintleman."

John and his wife, Honora Meara (O'Meara) had nine sons and it was difficult to sustain them all on the small landholding. After John's death on April 5, 1824, at age sixty-seven, his wife and sons buried him in the cemetery overlooking Lough Derg, a picturesque widening of the Shannon River, and seriously considered emigrating to North America where land was plentiful.

In the spring of 1826, the O'Gradys left Ireland. Somehow the family managed to scrape together

Brothers Martin (1836–1920) and William (c. 1845–1918) O'Grady. Martin was one of the first to settle in Hagarty Township in the late 1850s.

enough money to pay the passages of their mother, eight of the sons—the eldest two of whom had wives—as well as two infant children for a total of thirteen. Judith Darcy, the wife of Michael O'Grady, gave birth to their third son, James, shortly after they arrived in Montreal in June 1826.

After approximately two weeks in Montreal, the O'Gradys travelled up the St. Lawrence River by boat to Prescott. From there they trekked across country to Perth, a military settlement established in 1816. At this time free land grants were no longer available, having been abolished the year before, so the O'Gradys soon found jobs building the Rideau Canal for Colonel By so as to raise money to buy land. Unfortunately, John, the sixth O'Grady son, drowned in 1827 while working on the canal.

In 1828, Michael O'Grady petitioned for a tract of land for himself and his six brothers, but it appears that this request was not granted although the petition was supported by Colonel By. Then on March 19, 1828, Daniel O'Grady, the third eldest son, purchased 200 acres of land in Nepean Township. His two older brothers, Michael and Henry, combined resources and purchased approximately 100 acres of land on the Rideau Front on July 27, 1830. On November 25, 1831, the fourth son, James, purchased 100 acres on the Ottawa Front. In turn, Daniel helped establish his brothers Thomas and Roddy, by selling them part of his land. Living on another part of this same lot was another brother, William.

The original O'Grady family expanded greatly in their first couple of decades in Canada. Six of the eight brothers who had come out (one died a bachelor and the other drowned) had married and fathered large families ranging from eight to fourteen children, the majority of whom lived and died in Nepean Township.

The exception was the family of the fifth son, Thomas, who had married Margaret Spaine around 1835 and had the largest family of the eight brothers. His eighty-acre farm in the Township of Nepean was the birthplace of his fourteen children—seven sons and seven daughters. Today, part of it is in the Ottawa Greenbelt and part in Bells Corners. Yet, his land was poor, flat and swampy, and there was no adjoining or neighbouring land available on which his seven sons could hope to establish their own farms.

Thomas's son, John, with a couple of his brothers, and several other Nepean lads found jobs on the rivers as raftsmen in the square timber trade. No doubt on their treks up the Ottawa and the Bonnechere Rivers they became aware of the free land being opened up in Renfrew County.

At some point in the late 1850s, they squatted in the unsurveyed hills of Hagarty Township. Although the patriarch of the family was registered on the lot that John eventually homesteaded, it is not known whether Thomas ever actually moved from Nepean to Hagarty, for he was buried in the cemetery at St. Patrick's Church, Fallowfield, on September 9, 1865, at the age of sixty-two. However, he probably did spend time establishing his sons in Hagarty for two of his children were married in Brudenell: Anne, his sixth child, on April 26, 1863, to Joseph Doyle; and John on May 11, 1864, to Mary Jane Lavoies.

After her husband's death, Margaret O'Grady brought the younger children to the wilderness of Hagarty and watched as one by one they married their neighbours' children. Only her eldest daughter, Sarah, remained in Nepean Township with her husband Owen Hammill on her father's eighty-acre farm.

Unfortunately, Margaret had to bury two of her children shortly after their arrival in Hagarty. Bridget (1847–67) was the first of the O'Gradys to be laid to rest in the Brudenell Graveyard. She was joined by her brother Henry, the third of the seven brothers, who died on March 4, 1871,

Our Lady of Angels Church (formerly St. Mary's Church), Brudenell, the O'Grady family church. Many of the family are buried here. *Sketch by Shirley Mask Connolly.*

when he fell from a wagon of loose hay and suffered a fatal head injury. He left behind a young widow, Winnie Costello, whom he had married in 1866, and two young children. He was only thirty-one. Henry had settled on Lot 22, Concession A, and after Winnie married Jack Sullivan on January 16, 1884, it became known as the Jack Sullivan place. Part of this farm remains in the Sullivan family to this day.

Margaret O'Grady (1852–1933) and her husband Thomas Daly (1841–1932). Their daughter, Sarah, married William McCarthy, who established McCarthy Motors in Killaloe.

The family worshipped in St. Mary's Church (now called Our Lady of Angels) at Brudenell and continued to live in the hills of Hagarty, clearing and farming the land of Concessions A, 1, and 2. Soon many grandchildren were added to the ranks and, because of the sheer numbers, the area became known as the O'Grady Settlement, in honour of the seven brothers and six sisters who pioneered here.

The early O'Gradys contributed in many ways to the development of the area. John became the first reeve of the combined townships of Hagarty, Sherwood, Richards, Burns and Jones. He was also the first postmaster of the township with his house bearing the mailing address of Emmett, after a famous Irish patriot. He served as the justice of the peace and recorded the census return of 1871 for Bonnechere (Hagarty).

Several years after John's death, his brother Con became the reeve and, in 1891, took the census for Hagarty and surrounding townships. Martin, the second son, was a pathmaster for many years, as was his brother, William.

Of the six daughters who came to Hagarty, only three had children: Anne Doyle, Margaret Daly and Catherine Kerwin. Bridget died young, while Elizabeth (McNamara) and Honora (Balkwell) married, but remained childless.

Martin was almost thirty-six in 1873 when he married Catherine, the daughter of Mr. and Mrs.

Martin Daly of the Opeongo Line. Her father ran a "stopping place" on the Line and his home housed the first township council meetings, and no doubt countless other business and social transactions, too. Martin and Kate O'Grady had ten children. Their farm was taken over by their son John and his wife Kate McMahon, who remained childless.

In the past century, the O'Gradys of the O'Grady Settlement Road in Hagarty Township have moved far beyond the borders of this township. Some have even returned to Ireland to retrace the path of their ancestors. The last O'Grady moved out of the O'Grady Settlement in 1974, but we are reminded of the family's tenure in this area every time we take a drive down the dirt road that bears their name.

Elizabeth O'Grady (1857–1922) and her husband Martin McNamara (d. 1928). They had no children.

INFORMATION

FOR

INTENDING SETTLERS

ON THE

Ottawa and Opeongo Road,

And its Vicinity,

BY

T. P. FRENCH,

#17

Crown Land Agent,

PUBLISHED WITH THE APPROVAL OF

THE HONORABLE JOSEPH CAUCHON,

COMMISSIONER OF CROWN LANDS.

AND

THE HONORABLE P. M. VANKOUGHNET,

PRESIDENT EXECUTIVE COUNCIL AND MINISTER OF AGRICULTURE.

OTTAWA, CANADA WEST,

1857.

T.P. French was appointed agent for the Opeongo Road in September 1855 and established an office in Mount St. Patrick, and later Clontarf, for the purpose of locating settlers along its line. By the end of 1858, approximately 200 families—more than two-thirds of them Irish—had obtained location tickets and settled along the Opeongo.

Petawawa Waterfront at the Turn of the Twentieth Century

by Ann McIntyre
Chair, Petawawa Heritage Committee

When you look at Petawawa Point today, you see a sandy beach, a concession booth, a boat launch, and a family picnic area. It is hard to imagine that there was a time when steamboats pulled into a large dock, passengers hurrying to get on board, supplies stacked on the dock ready to be loaded and taken up or down river, and goods being dropped off for local distribution. This area was to have been the town of Petawawa.

With the growth of the logging industry and a need for transportation and supplies, Petawawa's waterfront grew rapidly. A wharf was constructed to accommodate the docking of three large watercraft. As well, passenger and light freight boats docked at the wharf daily carrying passengers and supplies between Rapides des Joachims and Pembroke along the Ottawa River. They were the S.S. *Oiseau* (oh-e'-sew), the *C.B. Powell* and the *E.H. Bronson*. These three steamships were the pride and joy of the Ottawa River with the *Oiseau* getting the nod for being the most popular and prestigious. The *Powell* and *Bronson* were rugged paddlewheelers and were used solely for hauling log booms. On the other hand, the *Oiseau* carried both passengers and freight on daily return runs that started in Pembroke with a stop at the Petawawa dock.

The skipper of the *Oiseau* was Captain Tessier. Mrs. Lucas ran a refreshment stand on the boat and every kid's favourite soft drink, chocolate bar, and ice cream were available for purchase. Many loggers took advantage of moonlight sailing trips with their wives or sweethearts.

By 1870, a survey to lay out the town of Petawawa took place. The site chosen for this survey was the area referred to as "The Point," where the Petawawa River empties into the Ottawa River.

Petawawa Point had become a very active centre before the turn of the twentieth century due to the large logging industry and the docking of the steamboats. Therefore, it was an ideal area to lay out a town.

The waterfront area quickly took on other activities. In the 1800s you could find the McLean Hotel, more commonly referred to as the Dew Drop Inn, which was owned and operated by Jack W. MacLean. The McLean Hotel was a stopover for the men transporting supplies and the loggers going up to the logging camps on the Mattawa Road.

Petawawa Point was home to a popular dance hall that subsequently became the R.J. Booth family cottage. A sawmill owned by James Davis stood at the end of River Road, where the Johnston cottage now stands. Many of the local men worked here, including Mr. Ed Charette, who still resides in Petawawa.

The *Oiseau* sank in the late 1920s and it is believed that the Murphy Ferry was constructed using parts salvaged from her.

With the sinking of the *Oiseau*, the romantic era of the steamboats was almost over and the town of Petawawa was beginning to shift up to Kings Road/Highway 17, which is now known as Petawawa Boulevard.

"This route is one of the utmost difficulties for the first forty or fifty miles, the river being, as far as the level country, almost a constant succession of rapids, which cannot be ascended in less than seven days, by a light canoe in the dry season, and is hardly ever attempted at any other time."

— Alexander Shirreff, explorer of the Ottawa River, 1829, on describing the Petawawa River.

Petawawa waterfront at the turn of the twentieth century. *Photo courtesy of the Champlain Trail Museum.*

The Military Camp at Petawawa

by Colonel John Gardam (Ret.)

When I was asked to write a piece on the history of the Petawawa military camp, little did I realize that this would not be an easy task.

The military historical researcher at CFB Petawawa, Mr. Aaron Faulkner, had just begun to research such a history. He sent me three incomplete documents which form the basis for what you will now read.

In 1982, a lieutenant by the name of J. Lycon produced the most helpful document on the subject. In her brief history on the base, she explains that Petawawa has a long military tradition reaching back to May 1686, when Chevalier des Troyes led a hundred men up the Ottawa River to capture the English fur trading posts on the Hudson Bay.

CFB Petawawa takes its name from the Petawawa River. Although there is no consensus on the origin of the name Petawawa, according to one legend, it is derived from the Algonquin word "Petwewe," which means "where one hears noise like this," referring to the sound of water.

It is believed that early French explorers used a trail or route through this area, called the Mattawa Trail. Parts of it still exist on the base, although it is now referred to as the Mattawa Road.

The site of CFB Petawawa was originally a German settlement. German Lutheran pioneers migrated here around 1875, carving out of the wilderness a new home and community in hopes of finding freedom and religious licence. Several place names stand as reminders of these early German settlers: Behnke Wood, Jorgens Lake, Radke Hill, Gust Point and Baehstadt Road.

At the end of the Boer War in 1902, Canada's interest in national defence took on a more significant importance. The urgent requirement for an artillery training ground prompted the Minister of Militia and Defence, Sir Frederick Borden, to search for a suitable site. It was imperative that the new training ground be able to accommodate the long-range guns. The Department of Militia and Defence was forced to give serious thought in the fall of 1904 to acquiring suitable land for a central training area, accessible to the militia of Eastern Canada.

An inquiry was made that same fall as to the possibility of leasing Crown lands in the Petawawa area, in the event it was chosen. The following summer, the Chief of General Staff inspected three sites for the campgrounds and made his report on the following locations:

- in the vicinity of Petawawa, County of Renfrew, Ontario
- in the vicinity of Barry's Bay, County of Renfrew, Ontario
- near Kazuabazua, County of Wright, Quebec

On November 2, 1905, Earl Grey, the Governor General of Canada, signed an order-in-council empowering the Minister of Militia and Defence:

> "(To) acquire as a site for a Central Camp ground, whether compulsorily or as a result of negotiations, the land generally described as bounded on the South by the South Branch of the Petawawa River to its junction with the Ottawa; on the North, the boundary line between the 8th and 9th Concessions of the Township of Wylie and the right-bank of the Chalk River to its junction with the Ottawa; on the East, the Ottawa River (Allumette lake), and on the West, the Western boundary of the Townships of MacKay and Wylie, all lying in the County of Renfrew, Province of Ontario."

By 1911, the Department of Militia and Defence had purchased 150 properties from settlers totalling 22,430 acres. On March 20, 1908, by virtue of an order-in-council, Crown lands were assumed "in the right of the Government of Canada for the defence of the Country," under the authority of Section 117 of the *British North America Act*. The Crown lands consisted of 52,000 acres belonging to the Province of Ontario. As of September 1916, the total cost was $384,958.91

> ***"On the fifth of May [1686], we left after mass, to go to the portage at the end of la riviere creuse [deep river] . . . one sees on the north shore . . . a high mountain whose rock is straight and very precipitous, the middle a black wall. Perhaps that is why the Indians make here their offerings, throwing arrows over, to the end of which they attach a little bit of tobacco. Our French are accustomed to baptise at this place those who have not previously passed it. This rock is named l'oiseau [bird] by the Indians and as some of our people did not wish to lose the old custom of throwing themselves in the water, we camped below the portage [Des Joachims ."***
>
> **— Chevalier de Troyes, 1686, report on journey up the Ottawa River.**

Both Lieutenant Lycon and the *Army Historical Section Report of 1960* recall an event of national importance.

On February 23, 1909, J.A.D. McCurdy became the first man to fly an aeroplane in the British Empire. This flight took place at Baddeck, Nova

Scotia, aboard the *Silver Dart*. The *Silver Dart* proved so successful that McCurdy and his associate, F.W. Baldwin, received permission from the Canadian military authorities to demonstrate their aeroplane at Petawawa in the presence of military observers. In late July 1909, McCurdy and Baldwin took up their quarters at Petawawa Camp and on August 2, the *Silver Dart* was flown for the first time for military purposes. However, a fourth flight proved the *Silver Dart*'s last, as the plane was badly damaged in a crash. McCurdy and Baldwin suffered only minor cuts and bruises.

The Petawawa trials were well publicized. In addition to the *Silver Dart*, it was disclosed that the *Baddeck I*, also built by McCurdy and Baldwin, would be flown as well.

With the demise of the *Silver Dart*, the *Baddeck I* was flown for the official party from Ottawa on August 12. The party included Colonel Eugène Fiset, the Deputy Minister; Major-General W.D. Otter, Chief of General Staff; Brigadier-General D.A. MacDonald, the Quarter-master-General; Rutherford and Maunsell. This would be the *Baddeck I*'s first flight.

The official party left after only one flight, although Baldwin and McCurdy continued their trials. However, on the following day, August 13, the *Baddeck I* met with a fate similar to the *Silver Dart*. The aeroplane crashed and was badly damaged. Fortunately, McCurdy escaped with only bruises. The remains of both planes were shipped back to Cape Breton to be salvaged.

The First World War only receives a few, albeit important lines in the *Historical Section Report of 1960*.

From December 1914 to May 1916, the Petawawa area was used as an internment camp and, during the winter 1915–16, the Russian government was permitted to use the range for testing shells. Effective January 1, 1916, the area became a separate military district known as Petawawa Military District. In May 1916, a camp for artillery units was established for the artillery units of the 4th Canadian Division. In June 1918, in addition to an artillery camp, an infantry concentration camp was opened as a rest camp to accommodate overseas infantry reinforcements en route from Western Canada. From 1916–18, it was operated as a military establishment and 10,767 Canadian troops trained at the camp.

Lieutenant Lycon also provides insight to the internment camp and the Russian involvement in artillery shell testing, plus an interesting story about Chinese coolies.

Petawawa Military Camp was used as an internment camp for 750 German and Austrian prisoners of war, December 1914–May 1916.

They occupied various buildings that had been used by the militia in peacetime. During their internment, the POWs were employed at road cutting, timber felling and ground clearing.

Also at this time, three-inch shells manufactured in camp by the Canadian Car and Foundry Company were being tested by the Russians. In preparation for the tests, much work was required on the range. Approximately 256.5 acres had to be cleared, of which 108.5 acres needed to be grubbed and ground-levelled. This work was originally intended to be carried out by prisoner labour, but because of trouble with prisoners and the urgency of the work, civilians were employed and large quantities of explosives used.

Seven buildings were constructed by the Canadian Car and Foundry Company for the Russians during the tests: two cottages used as married quarters, a garage, a general office, a laboratory and magazine, a small storage building, and a ballistic building. It is believed that 2 Mons Road was one of two cottages used as quarters. It is the only survivor of the seven buildings. The Russians left Petawawa in February 1917.

The internment camp closed May 1916 and a camp for artillery units of the 4th Canadian Division was established. *The Pembroke Standard* reported on September 12, 1917, that some 3,000 soldiers were under canvas in Camp Petawawa. It was further noted that "The training camp is the best on the North American Continent. In conversations with various officers who have returned from France, they claim there is nothing over there to equal this camp."

A total of 2,288 Chinese "coolies" were detained for a week in August 1917 at Petawawa until transports could be arranged to take them to France. The "coolies" were quartered in what was known as the West Camp, last used in 1914. Before it was habitable, it was necessary to repair the plumbing, latrines, ablution tables, and water supply.

The Chinese were employed making improvements to the camp. The following is an excerpt from the camp engineer's report.

> "The men are distributed approximately as follows: over 500 lowering water-mains in the General Camp below frost, over 200 clearing-up bush around camp for prevention of fire. The balance were employed renewing beds of septic tank and filtering system, gathering and breaking stone for roads, grading roads, spreading manure and generally improving Camp. Total 2000 labourers. During their stay they were supervised by four Canadian Expeditionary Force Batteries."

Petawawa Camp came into its own in the Second World War when it became the training area for artillery and engineer reinforcement. In 1942, there were more than 12,000 troops stationed there. Lycon explains that, as in the previous war, Petawawa served as an internment camp. Officially known as Internment Camp No. 33, it was located at Centre Lake, the site of the relief camp abandoned in 1935. Internment Camp No. 33 opened in September 1939, although no accommodations were available at Centre Lake. The interned aliens stayed under canvas until proper buildings were constructed. Lieutenant-Colonel Pense, who founded the Veterans Guard of Canada, was appointed the commandant. The Petawawa Internment Camp was used for German and Italian civilian internees, September 1939–July 20,1942.

After being a separate military district during the war, Petawawa Military Camp returned to being a subordinate of Military District No. 3 in January 1946. The following year, training of militia units resumed. Regular army components returned to Petawawa in 1948, when the Royal Canadian Dragoons and the 1st Battalion Royal Canadian Regiment were transferred there.

Units of the Special Force, earmarked for service in Korea, were concentrated at Petawawa before going to the United States for departure to the Far East in the early 1950s.

This brings to a close one person's attempt to record the early history of a military presence at Petawawa.

Was Wilno Once Called Princetown?

by Shirley Mask Connolly

Many visitors to Wilno, Ontario, assume that the Polish people of the area are descendants of those who originated in Wilno, Poland (now Vilnius, Lithuania). However, none of the original Polish settlers in Renfrew County had any connection to the namesake town. Most came from West Prussia, southwest of Gdansk—the Kashubs—while a smaller group had origins in the Austrian-occupied portion of southern Poland.

The name Wilno was given to the first post office in the Renfrew County community not because of the Polish inhabitants, but in deference to the parish priest there at the time. Apparently, Father Ladislaus Dembski was born in Wilno, Poland. Father Dembski stayed in the Canadian parish of St. Stanislaus Kostka for approximately twelve years, faithfully ministering to the needs of his Polish parishioners, meticulously recording their baptisms, marriages and burials, before abruptly and mysteriously disappearing from the scene in 1892. Some said he went to Brazil.

However, despite the fact that his tenure was short in Renfrew County, the name Wilno was here to stay.

Wilno, c. 1901. *MacNamara Collection, Provincial Archives, Toronto.*

It has been suggested that Wilno was once called Princetown and this name certainly seems plausible. Adam Prince was the first postmaster, Polish schoolteacher and merchant in the area, but in those days there was no town on the present day site of Wilno.

In 1885, when the first post office opened up in Adam Prince's home located high in the hills of Hagarty Township, the Polish Settlement was nothing more than a farming community with a small log church dedicated to St. Stanislaus Kostka and a couple of hundred Polish people of mainly Kashubian origin scattered about the countryside. Only when the railway pushed its way through the Wilno Pass in 1894 did a village begin to grow. By that time, the name Wilno had been in existence for almost a decade. There is evidence, however, that back in the 1880s, Adam Prince's establishment was central to the community, second in importance only to the church. Not only was it the post office and store, but it housed council meetings for the United Townships of Hagarty, Sherwood, Richards, Jones and Burns, beginning on February 11, 1887. By 1888, the council minute book refers to "the Council Rooms at Adam Prince's," and council met their regularly.

There can be no doubt that Adam Prince made a mark on the settlement. When he died in January 1933, *The Eganville Leader* ran several obituaries paying tribute to the man, with such glowing descriptions as:

> "An outstanding personality in the western part of the county . . . he exercised great influence among his Polish compatriots who settled in the townships of Hagarty, Sherwood, Richards, Jones and Burns. . . . He was an ardent Conservative and where the fray was hottest, there the redoubtable Adam Prince could be found.[1]

> "His services as an interpreter were often required and his advice frequently sought in many matters by the large Polish community where he was always considered a leader."[2]

In fact, Adam Prince was so well known that his demise was mourned way beyond the boundaries of the Polish Settlement. A writeup penned by a reporter identified by the initials R.A.J. appeared in *The Ottawa Citizen*. Although marred by several obvious errors, the piece paints a dramatic portrait of the man and his life:

> "Long before the raucous screech of the locomotive echoed through the rugged hills and deep valleys of Wilno, the late Adam Prince was there. He was the pioneer, he blazed the trail and in the end he was the patriarch and the prophet in whose rich philosophies the Polish people of Renfrew county outposts manifested every confidence.

> "Adam Prince was just a boy when he left his unpretentious home situated within site of the historic Duchy of Warsaw and amid the wild unsettled and almost uncharted upper reaches of what eventually became Renfrew county, he established himself, he found new freedom from the Slavonic yoke that had for years been strangling his motherland. He became something of a sympathetic czar, a kindly sort of authority. He it was who suggested the name 'Wilno' for his home community. He established a business that assumed no mean proportions, his family sunk their roots deeply in the soil, and all the while this man who had broken virgin soil and felled the giant timbers was spreading his influence throughout the land until almost

Family of Adam Prince (front row, second from right) and Rose Pokrofska (back row, far left). Son Alexander is sitting to the right of Adam. The Princes' other children included Mary Ann (Mrs. Frank Pabubiski), France (Mrs. Thomas Cybulski), Mick, Tessie (Mrs. Michael P. Prince), Catherine (Mrs. Frank Shulist), Bronis (died in infancy), John J. Thomas, Rose (Mrs. Victor Cybulski), Ambrose, Flossie (Mrs. Stephen Vasiloff), Walter (died at age six), Agnes (Mrs. Thomas Gutoski), and Maximilian. *Photo courtesy of Danny Prince.*

everyone from the headwaters of the Madawaska to the sea knew something of the forceful character who in his day was ready and rough and honest."[3]

In reality, Adam Prince and his parents, Adam Princ/Prinz Sr. and Francesca Burant/Burandt, and his brothers and sisters left the small farm village of Kalisz, West Prussia, located in the Parish of Lipusz in 1868 when he was a boy of thirteen. In 1884, Adam married a Kashubian girl in Renfrew, by the name of Rose Pokrofska. They had a family of fifteen children and lived at what most certainly became known as Prince's Corner, at the intersection of today's Highway 60 and Church Street. Adam eventually built a big home across from the store, the only brick house in the community other than the Catholic church rectory. The house burnt during the winter of 1932. Later the store was bought by the Department of Highways and torn down so as to widen the road, leaving little left to remind us of Prince's Corner other than the stories of the old-timers.

The old log store faced westward, with a big front room and an upstairs office. It was a place that was always teeming with activity. Some recall hearing about the night someone tried to dynamite the old store on May 23, 1918.

> "An exaggerated report reached Eganville yesterday morning to the effect that the home, store and outbuildings of Mr. Adam Prince of Wilno, had been dynamited and destroyed. The facts were, however, that at one o'clock on Thursday morning a loud report disturbed the slumbers of residents in the locality. Investigation revealed that an explosive had been placed under one corner of Mr. Prince's store and considerable damage resulted. Mystery surrounds the occurrence and the identity of the guilty person or persons is unknown."[4]

It was generally thought that the deed was perpetrated by some of the local lads who did not appreciate Prince's fervent patriotism. When conscription was enforced during World War I, Adam allegedly informed the government military tribunal of the possible whereabouts of several conscientious objectors hiding out in "them there hills," much like the American draft dodgers a half-century later. Adam Prince was also an avid proponent of the Canadian Kashubs joining Haller's Army and fighting for Poland.

Eventually Adam's son, Alexander, took over the business, but located his store "downtown" on the southeast corner of the Hagarty–Sherwood town line. Both Prince stores are long gone, but the mercantile tradition continues today on the Round Lake Road side of Pembroke where Alexander's son and Adam's grandson, Danny Prince, operates a general store and post office.

Florence Lorbetskie, Adam's granddaughter, is the only member of the family still living in Wilno, just a stone's throw from where Adam's house once stood. The only Prince with a business in Wilno is Alfie Prince of Prince's Power Tools. Yet Alfie is not a descendant of Adam, but of the very first Prince family to emigrate to Canada in the summer of 1858, ten years before Adam's family. Alfie's ancestor, Anthony Prince, came from the same village in Poland as Adam's father, but the two were not brothers (although probably related). T.P. French, the Crown land agent at the time, indicated in his records that of the first fourteen Prussian-Poles to locate on the Opeongo Line in September 1859, only Anthony and his two eldest sons toughed it out in the bush. The rest of the group returned to Renfrew until the following spring. Anthony's son, Mikolaj, assisted French with transcribing the difficult Polish names. This family of Princes also deserves to be recognized for their contribution to the establishment of the Polish Settlement.

Danny Prince, grandson of Adam and owner/ operator of Danny's Hardware and Grocery, Pembroke. *Photo by Shirley Mask Connolly*

The name Princetown was mentioned by Brenda Lee Whiting in her book, *The Way it Was in the Ottawa Valley*,[5] and by Rev. Joseph Legree in his book, *Lift Up Your Hearts, A History of the Roman Catholic Diocese of Pembroke*.[6] Unfortunately, neither lists a specific origin for the name. However, there's a popular expression in the Wilno area, that "if you don't know, you Wilno," so maybe there is an old piece of paper somewhere, perhaps a letter, with the name Princetown clearly written on it. For although history is based on fact, it is also far from "being a closed book," dusty and dull, best left undisturbed. There are always a few missing pages. This may be one of them.

[1]*The Eganville Leader*, January 13, 1933.

[2]*The Eganville Leader*, January 27, 1933.

[3]Reprinted in *The Eganville Leader*, January 27, 1933.

[4]The Eganville Leader, May 24, 1918.

[5]"Wilno Named after Father Dembski's Birthplace," Article #10. 1992.

[6]Published in 1988.

Barry's Bay — Preserving Our Past

by Marion Atchison, Secretary-Treasurer

The Barry's Bay Railway Station Restoration Committee

A small but very important part of history has been preserved in our town.

Thanks to the dedication of a small group of people and the generosity of a great number of supporters, the wrecker's ball has not taken down

Alfie Prince in front of his store in Wilno. *Photo by Shirley Mask Connolly.*

our CN Railway Station nor Canada's last remaining wooden railway water tower on open struts.

The station itself was built at the turn of the twentieth century and the present water tower was built in 1943, but almost destroyed in 1975 when village council passed a resolution authorizing its demolition. One year later, the tower was designated a historical landmark thus saving it from ruin.

In 1989, the Barry's Bay Railway Station Restoration Committee was formed and fund-raising began. However, it was not until 1994 before restoration began with the help of an infrastructure grant. Materials were donated by local merchants and much volunteer work was relied upon.

Once the downstairs interior of the station was completed, the Ottawa Valley Tourist Association set up a tourist bureau inside. As time went by, we collected railway memorabilia to be displayed in the "waiting room" and later established an art gallery in the "baggage room."

Upon completion of the station renovations, our money was exhausted. However, in 1997, the

Ottawa Valley Tourist Association tourist information centre, located in the old Barry's Bay CNR station.

Railway Park Society was formed to clean up the property and once again we went to the people to raise funds to create what we so proudly recognize today as the Railway Station Park. This effort was completed without one cent of village tax dollars. An accomplishment we are so proud of.

Canada's last remaining railway water tower on open struts.

Now, with the station restored, we had to meet the challenge presented by the wooden water tower. Timing was perfect and we qualified for a millennium grant from the federal government. We received $24,000 in grant money and raised another $70,000 in cash and work-in-kind donations. The CNR also contributed $20,000 over a period of four years to the project.

The water tower was in dangerous condition at this point. A cooper and crew were hired and the first task undertaken was to shore up the whole structure. Within one month the tower was refurbished and the original water spout, with help from volunteers, was put back in place, making the structure complete once more.

Today you can walk on paved pathways in this beautiful park and view many of the donors' names marking trees, benches, light standards and the water fountain. The park is also the home of several pieces of memorabilia donated by local residents. A connection between the railway and the lumbering industry can be viewed when you look at the century-old Case steam engine on display. Seniors may recall seeing the quadracycle "Speeder" bicycle or the tool carrier on the tracks in the early 1920s.

Years of volunteer work have been poured into these projects, but we would do it all again to preserve our heritage. As you enter Barry's Bay from the east on Highway 60, you can tell we are proud of our town.

Pembroke

by Bill Higginson

As Pembroke grew from a police village to a town and then a separated city, it was known far and wide for its vast timber resources and its winning junior and senior hockey teams.

But now, as we enter the twenty-first century, a third resource has been added: the city has become a tourist destination point for the huge, powerful Ottawa River and as one of the gateways to Algonquin Provincial Park.

Never, even in his wildest dreams, would seventeenth century French explorer Samuel de Champlain have envisioned what would come to the area when he stood on the shores of the Ottawa between what is now Portage du Fort and Pembroke while he searched, unsuccessfully, for a water route to China. Indian guides brought him to this area by taking a shorter route via small lakes to Muskrat Lake and then to Morrison's Island.

While in this area he attended Indian "pow-pows," listened to native speeches, and spent time visiting Indian cemeteries. However, he finally realized his quest was fruitless and returned to Montreal. The Captain to the King of France in the Navy and Lieutenant to his Lordship, the Prince of Conde in New France, had failed to find a water route to the Orient.

Years passed. In 1828, Peter White, a timber operator who had holdings in the Ottawa-Hull region, founded a settlement in what is now the city of Pembroke. At that point, there were miles and miles of forest covering the region and, in May of that year, Mr. White began cutting the virgin forests. Eventually, a variety of timber companies were formed, including independent operators. Many, like Shaw Lumber, grew into successful lumber operations.

In 1846, a post office was established, a blacksmith opened a shop, town lots were being sold for as much as $80, and Thomas Pink opened a factory. The first steps to build a library were taken in 1875, the Canadian Pacific Railway began to build a line to Pembroke in 1876, and the village became one of the first communities in Canada to have electric lights on its streets. Pembroke became the county town and was a member of Renfrew County until former mayor, Angus Campbell, convinced the provincial government to declare it a separated city in 1971. In the meantime, industries like Steel Equipment, Eddy Match, J.R. Booth Ltd., Pembroke Shook Mills, Canada Veneer, Eaton's, several major banks, and KI International established themselves resulting in major growth, strong commercial development, varied and excellent education facilities, and the development of CFB Petawawa and Atomic Energy of Canada Ltd.

Many sports greats came from Renfrew County in general, and Pembroke in particular. One such team, the Pembroke Lumber Kings, became known for their winning ways until senior hockey's demise in the 1950s, and competed for the Allan Cup, the national Senior A championship, on two occasions. Today, the Junior Lumber Kings are still a team to be reckoned with in the Central Junior A Hockey League.

Today, Pembroke is expending strong efforts to attract new industry, retain what is already here, and develop a flourishing tourism program. New high-tech communications systems make it possible for large companies to locate in smaller centres and the city has joined the county in pressuring the province of Ontario to extend Highway 417 from Arnprior to Deep River, and beyond. And, if Samuel de Champlain stood amongst all the people who gather on the new Marina-Riverside Park complex in the centre of the city, he would be astonished and amazed—and, we hope, pleased.

> *"Thus we reached a lake six leagues long and two wide, so abundant in fish that the peoples of the region came here to fish. . . . Near this lake there is a settlement of Indians who till the ground and reap corn. The chief is named Nibachis, who came with his band to see us, marvelling that we had been able to pass the rapids and bad trails to reach them. . . . They showed me their gardens and fields, where they have corn. Their soil is sandy and therefore they are more inclined to hunting than to working the fields, in contrast to the Hurons ."*
>
> **— Samuel de Champlain, probably describing Muskart Lake, in Ross and Westmeath Townships, and the area covered by present-day Cobden. On June 7, 1613, Champlain lost his astrolabe near Green Lake, Ross Township. It was found by Edward George Lee in 1867.**

Dominion Forestry and the Petawawa National Forestry Institute

by Jennifer Mercer[7]

Located on Highway 17, just south of the village of Chalk River, the Petawawa National Forestry Institute—or PNFI as it was referred to locally—had its origins in 1917 due to the land expropriation process initiated by the Department of Militia in 1905 for the creation of a military training area. The Petawawa Forest Experimentation Station, also known as Dominion Forestry, came into being when the Forestry Branch of the Department of the Interior requested a tract of land in the Petawawa Military Reserve to manage for research purposes. It was agreed that the station would remain under the jurisdiction of the Forestry Branch, and fulfil its occupational responsibilities by providing forest fire protection services to the entire military reserve.

The station was concerned mainly with four guiding principles of operation: research, demonstration of forestry principles, provision of services to other federal agencies, and the management of its experimental forest. Silviculture, tree physiology, genetics, resilience to fire, and seed cultivation were the main research functions of PNFI. The station began in 1918 with the planting of the first permanent plot, and gradually grew to approximately 100 square kilometres, encompassing a substantial portion of the Petawawa Military Reserve. Well-aligned rows of coniferous trees, which can still be seen today along the highway, are testament to the success of the station's efforts throughout the years. Many local men worked for the station throughout its years of operation, and it gained notoriety among local residents when a prisoner of war camp was constructed within its limits in 1939. Prisoners detained at Camp 33 worked throughout the reserve cutting timber and constructing roads. The station's general foreman for most of its productive period was Isidore Clouthier, assisted by foreman Bruno Clouthier, Isidore's brother.

The station was later renamed the Petawawa National Forestry Institute, a facility that remained in continuous operation longer than any other in Canada. It began facing financial difficulties in the 1970s. By this time, it boasted a scientific complex and a tourist centre. The public was welcomed to enjoy the scenic roads that snaked through the reserve, and could stop at the visitor centre to gain a greater understanding of the station's functions and history. Fortunately for the institute and its employees, PNFI remained open despite a suggestion forwarded in the late 1970s that operations should cease in 1979; however, cutbacks soon resulted in layoffs, and the closure of the visitor centre. In 1996, PNFI was finally closed, and the land reclaimed by the Department of National Defence. Although the administrative centre and roadways are now closed to the public, the visitor centre was redesigned and reopened to visitors in the summer of 1996 with great success.

[7]Reprinted with permission from *Staying the Run—A History of the United Townships of Rolph, Buchanan, Wylie and McKay*. The Rolph, Buchanan, Wylie and McKay Historical Society, Deep River, Ontario. 1998.

The Atomic Age

by Jennifer Mercer[8]

During World War II, it was hypothesized that if uranium atoms were bombarded with neutrons, they would split and release a tremendous amount of energy. Today, we realize the many practical applications of this process, but during wartime, the focus shifted to weaponry. If this energy could be released in a controlled manner—for example, in the form of a bomb—it could be used to subdue the enemy on a scale that had never before been imagined.

Unfortunately, the race to master this developing science was not limited to the Allies. Whoever could produce this weapon first would certainly hold all the cards, as far as the outcome of the war was concerned. To facilitate the Canadian objective of creating this nuclear action, a joint laboratory was established with the British. The Americans chose to remain non-committal, despite initial efforts for a continent-wide co-operative venture.

National Research Laboratories organized the beginnings of the project from several Montreal facilities; the new objective was the design of a reactor to facilitate a sustained nuclear reaction. The United States finally agreed to assist the Canadian effort in the spring of 1944 in the form of an exchange of information and vital supplies, effectively cementing the decision to build the reactor that had been theorized and designed by Montreal scientists.

Several areas were considered for the project, with great consideration given to maintaining the secrecy and viability of the site. An area in Buchanan Township, just outside the village of Chalk River, was determined the most suitable, given its proximity to a ready supply of fresh water, its relative isolation from major industrial centres, and its accessibility to administrative and supply areas via the highway and railway. Defence Industries Ltd. was contracted to complete the design of the reactor and its support facilities, as well as the town where scientists and employees would be housed.

Located a few kilometres upriver from the site, the town of Deep River was established virtually overnight. Much to the delight of local residents in Chalk River, who still had no idea what was being built in their own backyard, many roadways were upgraded and paved, streetlights were installed, and phone service was established on a wide-scale basis. On the other hand, dozens of individuals whose property fell within the boundaries of the site had to be relocated.

In the fateful summer of 1945, it became evident to government officials and scientists involved in the project that the Americans were far ahead in their efforts to design a weapon based upon the splitting of uranium atoms. With the release of the first atomic bomb upon the citizens of Hiroshima, Japan, the implications of nuclear power became frightfully real.

Although the focus of nuclear research was centred on weaponry throughout the next few years, greater promise lay ahead by harnessing the same power as a source of usable energy. The construction of the nuclear reactor—named ZEEP for Zero Energy Experimental Pile—was completed on September 4, 1945. That day, ZEEP went critical, creating the first nuclear fission reaction in Canada, and launched the nation on its pursuit of peaceful outlets for nuclear energy research.

Truly, life in Canada underwent a tremendous transformation in the years following the development of nuclear power. A great time of prosperity followed the return of troops from war fronts. Industry and economic development were at an all-time high. New communities sprang up, and cities expanded towards the new ideals of suburban living. People everywhere were ready for change, and gladly discarded their old way of life in favour of the promise of the "Atomic Age." The potential of nuclear energy was thought to be endless.

In the 1950s, the media indulged its consumers with visions of a future based on the newly harnessed atom—nuclear-powered cars, planes, and even vacuum cleaners. The plant at Chalk River provided employment opportunities for families whose previous means of financial support had been based solely on harvesting their fields.

It was important to determine the effectiveness of the nuclear reactors that were designed at Chalk River. Thus, it was announced on March 24, 1955, that a small generating station would be constructed to assess the feasibility of reactors in the production of electricity. The Nuclear Power Demonstration site was a joint venture between Atomic Energy Canada Ltd. (AECL), General Electric of Canada, and Ontario Hydro, and was located in Rolph Township, just east of the newly constructed hydroelectric dam at Rolphton. From this site, any power produced by the station could be fed into the existing supply from the dam. Colombo Bros. of Toronto was contracted to excavate the site, which hired many local men to aid in the process. This project did not demand the same level of secrecy that had been so crucial during the construction of Chalk River Laboratories.

The reactor, which was the first to employ natural uranium and horizontal fuelling, became operational on June 4, 1962. It produced only 20,000 kilowatts of electricity, a mere fraction of that produced by the dam at Rolphton. However, it operated for twenty-five years before being closed and dismantled in 1987. The main training centre and offices were demolished in 1995; the sealed and monitored radioactive main reactor hall is the only visible reminder of the site's existence.

Today, despite the unpredictable future for AECL and its CANDU reactors, research at the plant continues at a steady pace, and the site is currently the largest single employer of township residents.

---

[8]Adapted with permission from *Staying the Run—A History of the United Townships of Rolph, Buchanan, Wylie and McKay*. The Rolph, Buchanan, Wylie and McKay Historical Society, Deep River, Ontario. 1998.

History of Mons Rebekah Lodge No. 203, Arnprior

submitted by Mrs. Audrey J. Taylor

In 2000, we celebrated the eightieth anniversary of the institution of Mons Rebekah Lodge No. 203 of the Independent Order of Oddfellows (IOOF).[9]

Looking over the earlier records we find the institution of our lodge was held in the town hall at the corner of Madawaska and Elgin Streets, Arnprior, on February 23, 1920. However, due to the Great Influenza Epidemic, not all candidates were able to attend the meeting. Our lodge was named Mons after the Battle of Mons fought in 1914, during World War I.

Charter Members of Mons Rebekah Lodge No. 203, instituted Februrary 23rd, 1920

Dr. MacGregor	Mrs. Lina Powell
D. Carmichael	Miss W. Munro
J.G.M. Jack	Miss A. Drysdale
M.J. McComb	Miss Laura Clements
R.A. Styles	Miss Della Watt
S.S. Tripp	Miss Violet Gauthier
A. Bremner	Miss B.K. Wallace
Florence M. Miller	Miss A.L. Bradwin
Mrs. Ada Whyte	Miss Robina Cavers
Mrs. Minnie Jack	Miss A.G. Wallace
Mrs. Beatrice Armstrong	Miss G.M. Wallace
Mrs. Alice Bremner	

Eventually we moved to the Oddfellows Lodge Rooms over Robertson's Variety Store on John Street. The club rooms and kitchen were on the second floor. The rooms were heated with big pot-bellied stoves and the custodian had to carry up the wood for very little pay, while the member closest to the stove had to keep the fire going. By the end of our meeting, the room was warm.

Our first Noble Grand was Miss Wilhimina Munro and our first Vice Grand was Mrs. Florence Miller, who was also our founder. Later during a Friendship Night, we gave Mrs. Miller the name "Mother of Mons." She was also the mother of Audrey Miller, a dedicated member of Hazel Lodge No. 40 of Ottawa, who served as president of the Rebekah Assembly, 1970–71.

We raised money for the upkeep of our lodge by holding card parties, dances, and box socials; catering dinners in the town hall (for 45¢ a plate!); and lending out our dishes and cutlery for a small charge.

Mr. James Jack was our First Degree Captain. He was very efficient in the work of our order. Many of our ladies have since filled this most important office. It requires a lot of work and memorizing. We are very proud of our Degree Team. They have exemplified our Degree work in many of the surrounding districts and at the Eastern Rallies, which are mostly held in

Kemptville, Ontario. We were also invited to Eureka Lodge No. 129 in Ogdensburg, New York, to participate in their rally, on May 1, 1977, to exemplify our Degree.

It was during Mr. Jack's years as Degree Captain that we wore our first long dresses. The four main officers wore beautiful pink, green, white, and mauve dresses, while the other girls wore white. This really added to our Degree work.

Many of our sisters have received the high honour of the Degree of Chivalry, while a number have been appointed officers at the Assembly Session in Toronto. In 1976, our officers served as Hostess Lodge at the Assembly Sessions.

In 1942, our brother Oddfellows of Vivian Lodge No. 146 bought the beautiful old building at 112 Daniel Street North and had it renovated. It became a beautiful building in which to hold our meetings. It was dedicated at a banquet held on April 26, 1945. Many dignitaries, Brothers, Sisters, and friends from the surrounding districts attended.

We had a beautiful lawn bowling club at the back of the lodge for a number of years, which was enjoyed by lodge members and townspeople. However, when our membership increased, we unfortunately had to close the club and make a parking lot.

In 1945, Mrs. Mabel Story suggested a PNG Club. Mrs. Louise McComb was our first president and Mrs. Elsie Cotie our first vice-president. This was mostly a social club and we met once a month, usually in members' homes. After our meetings, we made tea towels and tea cloths, and gave them to the Lodge. We also made aprons, etc., for sale on the Variety Table at our May Tyme Tea.

Today, we entertain and serve lunch once a year to our Senior Citizens Club No. 707 in the Lions Hall. We also make favours for the patients in the Arnprior hospital and give donations to charitable organizations. Our Humanitarian Organization lends wheel chairs, crutches, bed trays, etc., to those who need them, free of charge. Most, however, make a donation, which we use to keep the equipment in shape. We hold monthly dinners and serve hot lunches on Wednesdays for senior citizens, businessmen, and those just passing by.

In 1998, a very pleasant and happy afternoon was spent in the Grove Nursing Home, Renfrew, when two of our Sisters were honoured with seventy years of membership in Mons Rebekah Lodge No. 203.

During our eighty years, lasting friendships have been made, and we can look back on pleasant associations and happy times, as well as other times when a helping hand was extended or a kind word spoken in days of sorrow or trouble.

As members of our order, let us continue to cultivate a fraternal spirit and be ready at all times to carry on the work that lies before us. May the teachings of Rebekah Oddfellowship be uppermost in our thoughts and may we continue to carry on in the principles of Friendship, Love, and Truth.

[9]The IOOF is a fraternal organization dedicated to benevolent works in the community and was first established in Canada in the mid-nineteenth century. The Oddfellows, recognizing the need for "a woman's touch and her helpfulness in carrying out the principles of Oddfellowship," brought into being the Rebekah degree in 1851, founding it upon the principles of faithfulness, hospitality, purity, and dedication to the principles of the Order as portrayed by women characters of the Bible. By the 1870s, they had their own lodges.

Lines to Mount St. Patrick

by Charles Mair[10]

Oft have I wandered by the pebbly shore,
And in the woods have had mine own delight,
And quiet pleasure.
Far-seen expanses, both by day and night,
Have warmed my sight,
And caused my longing spirit to soar
From common sounds up to a lofty measure.

Yet never did I greet the clear sublime,
Until with patient steps I climb they steep,
And looked beyond
A thousand forests yielding music deep;
And saw the thunder leap
In mist from cataracts, nor heard their rhyme
Tired in dim distance though mine ear was fond.

Out o'er the pleasant villages I looked,
While morning swept the haze from meadows
wide.
And, far away,
In op'ning woods I saw where Bonnechère
brooked.
To swell great Uttwa's tide,
And where large streams grew small, and little
rills
Were dimmed from sight afar by distance grey,
Wedged in the heavens stood the dark blue hills.

What antique forms I wot lay undescried
Beyond those hills in lonely valleys deep
Sweet Fancy drew—
Of captive maidens weeping side by side,
Or fairy hermitages lost in sleep.
For there the distance blent with dim romance,
And clasped my thought away in regions old.
I saw the shadows creep
From ancient days, while dream-like forms anew
Bestrode the earth, and, in a waking trance,
Lived o'er again the wondrous age of gold.

O happy, happy mount, which doth extend
A wild outlying space for roving thought;
Spurning the plain
Where sorrowing eyes and rankling cares abide;
Where hapless men in weary tangle caught,
Narrow life's circumstance to purpose base;
Thee would I ever seek to ease my pain!
Nor long, while up the silent slopes I wend,
Or loll in idlesse on they swarthy side,
For Heav'n to take me from the summer days,
Away from thee to view Creation wide.

---

[10]Charles Mair (1838–1927). Born in Lanark, Ontario, he abandoned his medical studies at Queen's University in 1868—the same year his first volume of verse was published—to travel to Fort Garry and prepare confidential government reports on the rise of Louis Riel and the increasingly tense situation at the Red River Settlement. His vividly descriptive letters to the Toronto *Globe* both encouraged settlers to come West and antagonized the local French Canadians, Métis, and Hudson Bay Company officials with their derogatory characterizations. He was among those captured by Riel's forces during the first Riel Rebellion in 1869. He was a founding member of Canada First, the first nationalistic movement to form in Canada. Mair is also recognized as one of the first to poets write about Canada.

THEMS THAT BE ABOUT

The Scrapper

by Garry Ferguson

About the time my folks settled on schoolteacher as my future position in life, I decided to become the toughest son-of-a-gun in all of Renfrew County. I would be a better fighter than big Mike Leary had been in his day, and he was the best to ever come out of the Ottawa Valley.

There wasn't a scrapper around who could beat *him*, but the meanest still made the journey from lumber camps along the Madawaska and Gatineau to try. I sensed from the tales of old lumberjacks who hung around Granger's store in Tamarack the ferocity of those exciting battles.

"Gonna be a scrapper," I said to my grandfather one Sunday as he rocked on the verandah and surveyed his fields of ripening clover.

"Ya don't say." He shook his head. "Never figgered there was much gain in that kinda stuff. Now, schoolteachers, them's the people who git a steady wage. Don't mind ever hearin' about them gittin' their necks broke or their hands dirty doin' it neither."

"Never liked schools," I countered. "Anyways—you worked with Mike Leary. There was nobody could beat him, eh?"

Grandpa rubbed a weathered hand over his jaw scraped clean for church that morning and squinted against the afternoon glare. "Never met a man who didn't git beat eventually," he said just as I was about to repeat the question. "But Mike was tough. Smart too. Had a good head on his shoulders. Could've made a good teacher."

"He'da been great at knockin' the big lads silly when they stepped outta line," I added.

"Yaah." He ignored my interruption. "Worked with him on the river drives. I seen him manys a time, knock a fella kickin'. He got himself smashed up over the years, but usually his bouts didn't last long." Grandpa pulled his straw hat low on his forehead and stretched his legs until his heels rested on the verandah railing.

"Was it really true—you know—about fighters comin' down to Renfer to take him on?" I asked in an attempt to get him started again.

He sighed, scratched his leathery neck and said, "Yyaah."

I waited.

"You had to line up to get at him some Saturday nights—if you were that crazy. He finally took to stayin' around the farm to get away from the nastiness. Often said, I hear tell, that he wished he'd got the education to teach school. They still came lookin' for him though. One summer's day a big brute strode up to the Leary house and hammered on the door. He was after trouble."

I smiled. Grandpa would be difficult to stop once he was this far into a story.

"'I'm here after Mike Leary,' he rumbled to Mike's sister Mary, who answered the door. 'Is he here?'

"Now this Mary was big and rawboned, like all the Learys, but she was one handsome gal. Had red hair and blue eyes. Carried herself real straight and graceful like. Turned allotta heads—if you get my drift.

"'You'd best be on your way,' she warned, lookin' straight into a set of eyes that were too small for the resta the man. 'Mike feeds fellas like you to his hounds what are tied up out b'hint the bairn.'

"The lad scowled and clenched his teeth 'til she figured his jaw bone'd break.

"'I can beat any man between Ottawa and Deep River,' he snarled, curlin' his hairy paws into fists. 'I come a long way for this and I'll not be put off.'

"'Okay,' sez Mary. 'C'mon in and wait in the parlour. Mike's out, but he'll be home soon. Wipe your feet—and take your hat off.'"

Grandpa stopped talking while he unbuttoned the neck of his flannel shirt and unslung his braces.

"She tried talkin' to him, anglin' to find out if the fella was a professional scrapper," he continued after resettling himself in the rocker. "But he wasn't given to much talk.

"He kept lookin' at the new boots he was sportin' and swattin' dust off his store-boughten suit. Mary got the sneakin' suspicion that he might've dressed up jist to fight Mike. Even had his hair parted down the middle.

"'I spar with Mike myself—to keep him sharp you know,' she mentioned.

"He just sneered. By this time she was gettin' awful sore because of his bad manners, but she kept her temper down pretty good for someone who came from the Irish, eh.

"'Mike shoulda been here by now,' she told him. 'If he stopped at the tavern, you're in big trouble, Mister. He don't know when to stop if he's had a few.'

"His jaw relaxed and she saw the beggar smile behind his big moustache.

" 'It'll be a shame to see that nice suit ruint.'

" 'No feara that,' he snorted. 'Won't even get wrinkled. I'll make damn' sure she's all over in a big hurry.'

"Well! Mary said she felt like jumpin' up and tearin' his dirty eyes out, but she held her peace like a lady.

"He refused tea but accepted her offer to show him the place b'hint the house where Mike practised. She said she didn't get to likin' him any better when, on the way out, the clumsy beggar stepped a big dung tramper on the hem of her skirts.

"Anyways—blood sure flew that day."

Blood? Nobody bled in my imaginary fights. I hit them hard, but they went down just long enough to let everyone know I'd beaten them. We always parted as good friends.

My grandfather moved his chair to follow the creeping shade and seemed to lose his train of thought.

"Mike Leary really laid one on him when he got home, eh?" I prodded.

"No. That's not exactly how she happened," Grandpa said with a shake of his head.

My gut somersaulted then tried to squeeze its contents into my throat. Big Mike Leary had been beaten by a low-class bully. I tasted bile, the bitterness of defeat.

"The stranger was the man who finally licked Mike then." My voice was limp with disappointment. "Too bad. Darn! Too bad."

Grandpa continued to shake his head. "Naw. What happened, y'see, is that Mary talked him into tyin' on the gloves for some warm-up sparin'—with her. His new boots were like skates on the dry grass so the big oaf slipped and knocked her down. He flailed around, pawin' at the air like he was swattin' blackflies, then fell on toppa her. She pounded the snot outta him. Broke his nose before he figgered out which way to look. Almost bled to death before old Doc could get'm patched up.

"Nobody around here ever heard of him agin.

"You never know, eh. Could happen to you, too. It'd be a real corker, eh. Wastin' your life tryna get tough and then have the stuffin's knocked outta you by somebody's little sister. The shame—probably have to move to another country."

So, Mike hadn't been beaten by the stranger. My comfortable little world of blue skies and bloodless brawls righted itself. Its previous atmosphere of unpolluted certainty now, however, carried a faint scent of doubt.

"You know, Grandpa, I could teach—if I ever make it through grade three—and be a scrapper on weekends. Maybe as good as Mike."

"Well, I don't know. With a few more bags of flour under your belt, hopefully as good's his sister, but I like your idea. You're a pretty sharp little jigger. That's for darn sure. Probably already figured out that teachers learn the gift of the gab. That's why you never see them in a scrap. They can talk their way out of it."

I nodded as Grandpa pulled his hat a little lower and went back to watching the clover grow.

The Shanty Cook

by Garry Ferguson

I'd heard the complaints. Not until that night before matters finally got out of hand, however, did I get an inkling of just how ugly the mood among the lumberjacks at the Bear Creek logging camp had turned. The grumbling was always about one thing—Ned Towns the old cook.

I sidled toward Tom MacEwen, our foreman, as he rested on his bunk after supper. "I don't think nobody else's noticin', eh, but Cook's got his dirty ol' arse plunked down on the flour bag agin," I whispered.

"Hmm, so he has." Tom's even tone warned me that he wasn't about to get excited over my observation.

"Strikes me as odd though, young Willie," he confided as he yawned and rubbed his wind-burned face. "Y're the first I heard bitch about it all day, yet some're riled enough t'throw down their axes and head 'er out fur home."

Most of the men had gathered at the rear of our one-room shanty and, in the light of a smoking lantern, were listening to Jimmy MacLellan sing *The Jam on Gerry's Rock*. I moved closer to Tom, depending on the singing to keep anyone from hearing my complaint.

"Watch'm." I rolled my eyes toward Ned who sat like a contented turkey on a nest. "You'll see for yourself what makes me wanna stick my finger down my gullet and honk up the bread I jist et. He keeps liftin' one leg, eh. Now it might be all in my head, but I swear there's a little cloud of flour goes up b'hint him every time he does it."

"Well, I sure as hell kin understand how you feel, lad." Tom clasped his hands behind his head and spoke with enough sympathy in his voice to make me feel guilty for badgering him. "A young buck like yourself ain't developed a cast-iron gut yet. Wunst he fries up the dough it don't much matter anyway. But I gotta figger out sumpin' without sendin' the sawed-off little bounder into a rage. Got such a turble temper. Probly fly right off the handle and take 'er in his head to up and leave."

Tom seemed to bask in the reek of wet wool socks and wood smoke while hoarding warmth from our camboose fire against the cold he'd face tomorrow. He stretched hard enough to make me suspect he'd added a few inches to his five-and-a-half-foot frame.

"Far as I'm concerned," he continued, "Ned couldn't parboil shit for a tramp, but a bad cook's a helluva lot better'n no cook at all. I've let it be known that the man who flags him about sittin' on the flour bag is sure to be the same stupid bastard what's cooking the next meal. You'd do well to do some figgerin' on that."

I glanced in Ned's direction and noticed that he was staring through his pipe smoke in my direction. My heart leaped from walk to gallop but I tried to appear casual. His hat brim, sagging from age and the heat of too many cooking fires, cast a shadow over his eyes. In the dim light, it was difficult to determine if Ned's stare was really focussed on me. The weight of his drooping white moustache seemed to stretch wrinkled skin from his eyes to the corners of his mouth so I prayed that the scowl was a result of gravity, not displeasure.

He stood and tapped his clay pipe on the edge of the table.

I resumed normal breathing.

Ned stretched his braces and squinted down the front of his oversized trousers. I couldn't decide whether my older shantymates were pulling my leg or if Ned, in truth, did this to check his moggin laces. He turned away to some chore.

I looked back toward Tom. He was asleep.

Tom, a friend of my father's, had known me since I was born and when I'd finished all the grades at the log schoolhouse in Tamarack, gave me a break by hiring me as "cookie" or chore boy.

"Fourteen's a little young," he'd said, "but I got no fear becoz the lad's a dam' good worker." He had even allowed me to bring a couple beaver traps for some Sunday trapping—provided my mother didn't find out. The deep snow had ruined my chances as a trapper though, so the traps hung, unused, by the shanty door.

I wasn't aware of everything that went on among the lumberjacks, but the anger directed at the cook didn't surprise me. The hardships of a long, cold winter had soured many of us. Snowstorms, vicious enough to rip the skin from our faces, rode winds out of the north for days at a time. They smothered us, like giant blankets, cutting visibility to the length of a team and sleigh during daylight—less than that of an axe handle at night. Deer came silently out of the cedar swamps to feed at our haystack while we huddled in the shanty like louse-ridden pigs in a pen.

It should have been evident to even a youngster like me, though, that something rotten was brewing when the complaints ceased. I hadn't realized it, but we were in the calm before all hell breaks loose.

Daylight was still a long way off when we rolled out of our bunks next morning. Even the worst troublemakers settled chewing matches over socks and mitts in a half-hearted manner as though some other matter occupied their minds. Larrigans were laced on and the hands carried their breakfasts to their bunks. My morning grumpiness blinded me to sneaky glances at the flour bag.

Ned waited until everyone had filled his plate then decided, evidently, to take a rest. A thick cloud of smoke belched from his pipe and detoured around the hat brim on its way toward the roof. His shuffle toward the flour bag triggered a hush as much of the chewing and slurping stopped. The scuffle of his larrigans and the crackling of burning logs were the loudest sounds in the room. He sat down.

A muffled, metallic clank broke the silence a fraction of a second before a round hole opened under Ned's moustache and an ear-splitting bellow paralysed me. His pipe flew across the room and the hat went after it.

Faster than the beaks of two hungry woodpeckers, his feet beat a tattoo on the floor as he scrambled, inside a cloud of flour, to get off the bag.

I knew that the intensity of the tantrum shocked more than me, because I heard several metal plates and shanty mugs make "thunks" or "sloshes" as they slid onto the earth floor. Big men scrambled to make way for the shrieking little dervish who leaped with enough energy to make a Cossack dancer look arthritic. His speed gave an impression of several identical Neds doing some sort of wild square dance in the middle of a windstorm.

Ned's antics distracted me at first from the fact that his attention was directed toward something on the arse of his whipcords. In spite of bad light, even the slowest of us soon figured out that it was one of my beaver traps.

A burning log, kicked from the camboose onto the floor, sent up a shower of sparks just as he pried the trap loose and hurled it in my direction. I ducked and it crashed against the log wall.

The only permanent damage was another rip in Ned's pants, but he lit out down the unbroken sleigh trail anyway. Without snowshoes, he had about the same chance for survival as a useless rooster after the preacher's been invited for supper.

Tom harnessed a team to the jumper and went after Ned, but it took half a day to soft-soap him into coming back. Tom swore to him that he'd raised hell with the whole crew and torn a strip a mile wide off their dirty backs. That evening he called everyone, except Ned, to the stable and informed us, in no uncertain terms, what would be done.

Other than the culprits who had implicated me by using my trap, I alone was certain of my innocence, so I tried to play it safe. For the next few months I allowed no sneaky look or smirk to cross my face at mealtime. I kept my eyes lowered and tried to look humble for I realised that a riled cook is a dangerous person. Ned sat on his flour bag, smoked his pipe and watched us eat.

In spite of the tension, the remainder of the winter went well. We even began to compliment Ned on his baked beans, for we learned that to survive a winter in a logging shanty, everybody has to give a little.

The extra bag of flour, for which we all gave a little to buy as a seat for Ned, was left for the mice when we broke camp in the spring.

"No course of life can undermine the constitution more than that of a lumberer and raftsman. The winter, snow, and frost, although severe, are nothing to endure in comparison to the extreme coldness of the snow-water of the freshets, in which the lumberer is, day after day, wet up to the middle, and often immersed from head to foot. The very vitals are thus chilled and sapped; the intense heat of the summer sun, a transition which almost immediately follows, must further weaken and reduce the whole frame, and premature old age is the inevitable fate of a lumberer. But notwithstanding all the toils of such a pursuit, those who once adopt the life of a lumberer, prefer it to any other."

— John McGregor, a traveller and writer in the Ottawa Valley, 1832.

The First Devine Family

by Pat Devine

The first Devine family arrived at Ottawa in 1843 from County Sligo, Ireland. Of the five brothers and two sisters, four brothers eventually moved to Renfrew County, the first being Felix in 1845. He was employed as a clerk by Elias Moore and then Gerrard McCrea, who were lumbermen at Springtown.

Felix was elected reeve of the Township of Bagot and was a member of the Renfrew County School Board, serving as Superintendant of Schools for Bagot and other townships. In 1856, Felix opened a general store in Springtown with the help of his second brother, Patrick. In 1864, Felix and Patrick moved to Renfrew where they opened another general store. Felix was eventually elected to Renfrew Town Council. He passed away in 1890.

One of Felix's sons, F.M. Devine, became a lawyer and was elected mayor of Renfrew in 1904 and acclaimed in 1905. As mayor, he met with Prime Minister Sir Wilfred Laurier to urge the protection of the Montreal, Ottawa and Georgian Bay Canal. He and solicitor T.W. McGarry applied for more protection at the double railway crossings of the Canadian Pacific and Kingston & Pembroke (K & P) Railways. He served on the executive of the Millionaires hockey team.

In 1872, Patrick Devine opened a first class general hardware store formerly occupied by Felix. He and Alex Barnet were appointed as the Conservative portion of a delegation to interview the prime minister, Sir Charles Tupper, regarding the K & P Railway coming to Renfrew. In the 1890s, Patrick built the Devine Block on Raglan Street and a house behind on Plaunt Street, both in Renfrew. These two buildings still remain.

A third brother, John, and his wife Mary farmed at the Pinnacle before moving into Renfrew in the 1870s to work as Patrick's assistant in the hardware store.

A fourth brother, Andrew, his wife Mary Kenny, and infant son John arrived in Renfrew and settled at the Pinnacle to farm, where they had eight more children. Later, they moved to Renfrew and built a house on Hall Street.
One of Andrew's sons, Matthew, helped in the hardware store and when Patrick died in 1894, bought the business. He and E.J. McGarry, who owned a hardware store in Arnprior, became partners under the name of Devine and McGarry. Matthew married Margaret Ellen Fitzmaurice, one of six daughters of Michael and Johanna (Culhane) Fitzmaurice of Argyle Street. He and his new wife took residence in the home on Hall Street that his father, Andrew, had built. Matthew served as magistrate for Renfrew, while Ellen became the first president of the Renfrew Division of the Catholic Women's League in

The Devine Home, Hall Street, Renfrew. Patrick Devine and Bea (Devine) McGarry on balcony; Matthew Devine on porch; Andrew Devine on settee at right; Mary (Kenny) Devine on steps in between nuns.

1926 at St. Francis Xavier Parish. Together, they raised six children. The eldest, also named Andrew, joined the U.S. army in World War I, while Michael joined the Canadian army serving as a lieutenant in the 102nd Battalion with Captain John McCrea, who wrote *In Flanders Fields*. Felix was ordained a priest of the Jesuit order and served as chaplain for twenty years at Collins Bay Penitentiary, Kingston. He was also a purser at Regiopolis College, Kingston.

Andrew's daughter, Bea, worked as housekeeper for her Uncle Patrick, where she met and married T.W. McGarry, a solicitor in Renfrew who was elected M.P.P. for Renfrew.

Matthew Devine and T.W. McGarry built one of the first five cottages on Calabogie Lake in 1885, first travelling by wagon, then the K & P from Renfrew. Both the cottage and the house on Hall Street remain in the Devine family under the care of Philip and his wife Pat.

The Chanonhouse Family

by Isabel Hargreaves

Dr. John Chanonhouse practised medicine in Eganville, Ontario. In later years, he went to Barry's Bay by train for a couple of days about twice a month to see patients there. While there, he stayed at Drohan's (Balmoral) Hotel. It was at Barry's Bay that he suffered a fatal heart attack and died in his room at the hotel, having had a good breakfast. A loud thud was heard from above and he was gone.

Born in 1840 in Kingston, Ontario, to Captain Robert Chanonhouse and Mary Vallier, he was the second oldest of their seven children. His father was the high bailiff and captain of the Kingston police force. Captain Chanonhouse died in Kingston in 1870 and his wife died in Eganville at her son John's residence in September 1897, age eighty-seven.

The Children of Captain Robert and Mrs. Mary Chanonhouse

- Thomas Chanonhouse, died 1870, aged 33
- John Chanonhouse, M.D., died 1906, aged 66
- Henry Chanonhouse, died 1867, aged 25
- Robert Chanonhouse, born 1846
- Rebecca Chanonhouse, died February 1849 (20 days old)
- Mary Chanonhouse, born 1845
- Susanna Chanonhouse, born 1851.

Dr. John Chanonhouse graduated from Queen's University in 1861 and served as house surgeon at the Kingston General Hospital. In 1862 he set up practice in Douglas, Ontario; in 1864 he moved to Eganville.

He was active in various local politics and established the *Eganville Enterprise*, which did not succeed, and, in 1891, the *Eganville Star*. He was instrumental in establishing the local telephone system, bringing a branch of the Merchant's Bank to Eganville, and securing the fine stone bridge that spans the Bonnechere River at Eganville. He also erected a handsome brick block of buildings in the town. Dr. Chanonhouse and his family attended St. John's Anglican Church; he is buried in St. John's Cemetery. There are several other ancestors buried there, and I still like to visit at least once during the summer while we are at our cottage at Combermere.

Dr. John Chanonhouse married Susannah Davies (1837–1900) of Wilberforce; they had two daughters and two sons:

- Robert, a medical doctor (1866–1928)
- Annie (1868–87)
- Mary (May), who married Rev. Angus Ferguson, an Anglican minister
- John (July 1872–August 1941), a druggist in Eganville. He married Delia Sherreffs of Almonte.

Of John Jr.'s three children, Clarence Chanonhouse married Mabel Pearson of Eganville. They in turn had two children, John and Susan. John had two daughters: Agnes, who taught school at Runnymede Collegiate in Toronto for many years and never married; and Bernice, who trained and worked as a nurse before marrying Arthur G. Whyte. She spent most of her married life in Montreal. Bernice and Arthur had two children, Sandra (Sandy) and Peter. Peter has three children.

Dr. Robert Chanonhouse practised medicine in Richmond, Ontario, until his death in 1928. He married twice: Isabella (Dolly) Hudson (1868–1910) from Combermere, Ontario, and Margaret Reid from Purdy, Ontario (1872–1942).

During the years that Robert attended Queen's University to study medicine, he taught school at Deacon, Ontario, during the summer months. He also played the violin and, with other musicians in the area, performed at local dances and picnics. This is how he met his wife Dolly, who lived at the Hudson House, Combermere, which was owned and operated by her mother Elizabeth Dennison Hudson. Her father, John Hudson, had died at an early age in 1876, leaving his wife to raise nine children on her own.

THE FIRST

COUNTY COUNCIL OF THE COUNTY OF RENFREW

ELECTED UNDER THE COUNTY COUNCILS ACT, 1896 FOR 1897–98

Standing (l. to r.): James McAnulty, Pembroke (No. 1) Division; Edward Tuffy, Westmeath (No. 4) Division; S. J. Dempsay, Renfrew (No. 5) Division; R. . Scott, B.A., Inspector Public Schools; J. H. Burritt, County Solicitor; Jas. Craig, B.A., Renfrew (No. 5) Division; Archibald Foster, Pembroke (No. 1) Division; W. J. Johnston, Arnprior (No. 3) Division.
Seated (l. to r.): Thomas Maher, Brudenell (No. 7) Division; S. E. Mitchell, County Clerk; Thomas Heenan, Wilberforce (No. 2) Division; J. Chanonhouse, M.D., Warden, Wilberforce (No. 2) Division; John McEachan, Admaston (No. 6) Division; Alex. Morris, Co. Treasurer; Bernard Leacy, Admaston (No. 6) Division. Insert (left) James Bonfield, Brudenell (No. 7) Division. Insert (right) John Brennan, Arnprior (No. 3) Division. *Chas. N. Harding, Photographer, Pembroke*

Robert and Dolly had four children:

- Annie (1895; she lived only one day)
- Mildred Susan (1898–1965), who married Roy J. Henry and had no children.
- Isabel Clara (1901; she died at nine months from whooping cough. They had brought her from Richmond up to Eganville where the land was higher and the air much purer, but to no avail.)
- John H. (September 1896–November 1977).

John, my father, was born at Richmond and always said that he would not have lived had it not been for his grandmother, Elizabeth Hudson. He weighed only one-and-one-half-pounds at birth. He spent the day on the oven door, wrapped in cotton batten in a large wooden matchbox. For the first few months of his life, he spent the night on his grandmother's chest for warmth. His sister Mildred received the same treatment as she weighed only three pounds at birth.

John married Verna Ann Seabrook of Stittsville in 1932. They had five children:

- Isabel Chanonhouse Hargreaves
- Ann Chanonhouse McGuire
- Robert Chanonhouse (died October 1998)
- Nancy Chanonhouse Hill
- Helen Chanonhouse Schmidt.

I and my husband, John Hargreaves, live in the original cottage at Combermere, built in 1937 by my great-uncle Dr. William A. Hudson, a dentist from Albany, New York. My sister Nancy and her husband, Rev. Robert Hill, have a permanent home on the property, and my sister Helen and her husband, Heinz Schmidt, have another cottage on the property.

We have spent all of our holidays as a family in the Combermere area. This will be my sixty-eighth summer there.

My father had a 1936 Ford, which was packed to the roof in the back seat whenever we took a trip. It took all day to travel from Richmond to Combermere. The older children would find a spot to lie, and somehow there was room for the baby and dog. There were no seat belts in those days. Mother packed a lunch for us and we would stop at Arnprior, then go on to Eganville to visit Dad's relatives' graves, and back down the hill to the main street where Dad's uncle, John Chanonhouse, still had the drugstore and a soda fountain. My sister Ann, brother Bob, and I loved to run up and down the steps between the post office and my uncle's drugstore, which led to the street above. Uncle Jack and Auntie Delia had an apartment over the drugstore and a beautiful garden, which also went up the hill. I don't think the steps are maintained any longer.

Uncle Jack and Auntie Delia always made us welcome. They had wonderful ice cream cones at the soda fountain and Uncle Jack always made us very large cones. Mother dreaded the rest of the trip, because by the time we got to the big hill at Wilno, we were all sick. However, Mother was always equipped with paper bags, wash cloths and towels, and when we got to Wadsworth Lake on the Old Barry's Bay Road, we would stop to get cleaned up and wash out the towels and wash cloths for the rest of the trip. (No plastic bags in those days.)

Our first stop would be at the old hotel at Combermere to see Dad's aunts. We would stay with them for a few days, and then move on to find a place to camp. It became a bit noisy with, at that time, four children running up and down the hall at the Hudson House, so early in the morning. Mother and one of Dad's uncles would take the children out for a drive and swim so that the other guests could get some rest. It was when the fifth child arrived that they rented a cottage from Dad's cousin, Gill Waddington. This continued until my Dad built a cottage out on Long Lake in 1946.

We all have many happy memories of our vacations in the Madawaska Valley.

Town Crier

by Shannon Lee Mannion

Jack Lockwood, longtime owner of the Wood Works of Renfrew, stands at the ready in his front yard on Raglan Street. He is wearing an old-fashioned uniform that looks faintly military. The tricorn hat, the black and red tails and red cummerbund, coupled with tight white pants and black shoes with buckles, have a decidedly Georgian look. He is wearing his town crier costume and in celebration of the waning midsummers eve, he is about to set off his cannon. "Oye! Oye!" He pretends to read from a velvet-backed scroll as he lights the fuse.

Kaboom! Scorched and flaming paper disperses the length and breadth of the driveway as black smoke billows from the bore. The shot echoes across the gully not half a mile from the Renfrew fairgrounds. Jack stands in his driveway, charred match still in his hand, and beams at his wife of fifty-four years, Agnes Lockwood. She smiles back and says, "That was a good one."

Agnes is a willing participant in these shenanigans. It was she who tailored the town crier costume out of some unused party finery, fashioning the scroll from red velvet that had been an evening skirt. The two were born in 1921 and 1923, respectively, at the Renfrew Victoria Hospital, Jack as John Robert Lockwood, and Agnes, an

Oye! Oye! *Photo by Shannon Lee Mannion.*

only daughter for the Fishenden family. They both attended Renfrew Collegiate Institute, met along the way and married in 1947, a couple of years after Jack's three-and-a-half-year stint in the Royal Canadian Navy.

No doubt she is recalling other occasions the cannon has been discharged, happy occasions, such as her daughter Diane's wedding in 1982. Or the time she and Jack brought the cannon to the locks below the Château Laurier in Ottawa to start the pointer boat races on the Ottawa River. Or the times that the cannon played a pivotal role in their life at the cottage on Norway Lake.

The cottage has been in the family since Jack was ten years old and was originally jointly owned by his father, Fred Lockwood, and his friend, Harry Young. The property was bought seventy years ago from Jimmy Hamilton for the princely sum of $5—that's $2.50 each. A building, Twin Lodge, was erected and shared by scores of cousins over the years. However, since the mid-1960s, the cottage has belonged solely to Jack and Agnes. Jack's comment, "It fell into my hands and I renovated it." Now Jack's teenaged grandsons, John and Jamie, spend summer days at the cottage with their grandparents and parents, Bob and Lorraine Lockwood.

The cannon, built in the early 1980s, spent many summers at Norway Lake. It sat on the deck and, true to the British tradition of his ancestors, he held a ceremony every sunset whereupon he fired the cannon and lowered the flag. "We did this every evening at about the same time until a neighbour at the far end of the lake threatened to come over and spike the gun," he recalls, "I suppose it scared the bejesus out of them every night," he winks.

Jack Lockwood is not the only person in Renfrew who owns a cannon. In fact, it was Dr. Bill Burwell who initially provided Imbleau's Foundry with the pattern from which to build the quarter-scale British-style model. Imbleau's is mainly known for the manhole covers they produce, but as the oldest industry in Renfrew, they have cast many different things. Creating a cannon was not a tall order. Aware that the four-foot cast iron cannon might not be strong enough to sustain ongoing explosions, it was lined with a stainless steel tube of approximately quarter-inch thickness. Jack built the base out of solid red oak from the Wood Works and made the eight-inch wooden wheels using a bandsaw. A coat of black paint for the cannon and red for the carrier complete the piece.

Look closely and you will see the raised initials, ER II, at the base of the cannon. These commemorate the reign of the current monarch, Elizabeth II.

In preparation for firing the cannon, Jack first fills the barrel with a charge of gunpowder and then tamps newspaper wadding into place with a wooden ramrod. He inserts a fuse and lights it. As he readies the charge, he describes how one of the other cannon owners had once shot a flashlight battery from his cannon, and how another had put in a dead fish, to see if it would fly. There was even a time when someone filled their cannon with firecrackers and shot them into the air, hoping that the sparks would ignite them.

Kaboom! Jack in his town crier outfit turns, looks decidedly pleased with himself, and takes a little bow. As he tugs the cannon closer to the house, two youths descend from a car parked across the street. One has a camera. They are shy about asking, but they saw the cannon and colourful costume and wondered if they could take a photo. They are passing through town on their way home to Welland and have never seen anything like this before. Jack poses with the teenagers and they gleefully return to their car.

Jack retired from the Wood Works in 1986 and he and Agnes have since enjoyed several trips overseas. They've visited Scotland and other parts of Europe, but it is Russia in particular that Agnes loves. It is here that she bought several Fabergé-style eggs that join other mementos and objects d'art in their home designed by Burnstown ceramic artist, Richard Gill. They also indulge their passion for the theatre and try never to miss the Stratford and Shaw Festivals. If the National Arts Centre in Ottawa has an interesting theatre season, the Lockwoods are in regular attendance.

The family continues their long association with St. Paul's Anglican Church on Argyle Street. Agnes is quick to point out that the church is over 100 years old and that she has been a member for all but the first twenty years. "I was christened, confirmed and married at St. Paul's," she says. "And my children, Bob, Thom and Diane, were christened and confirmed there, plus Diane was married there." Agnes has the distinction of having been a member during every minister's charge since the church's inception. "Canon Quartermain was there for fifty-two years," she explains, "And this is how I have heard them all. Ken Rutter stands out in my mind but I also liked Doug Christie. He went on to Christ Church Cathedral, you know." She continues to help with the Ladies' Auxiliary whenever she can.

As for Jack, he was a dedicated businessman and he has turned this dedication to enjoying his retirement. If anything, life is more exciting. In the mid-1980s, he built an ultra-light aircraft at the second floor woodworking shop where, first, the Wood Works sash and door factory existed and, in later years, Thom made custom-designed, hand-crafted furniture. The ultra-light crashed shortly after takeoff and was summarily sold. (No injuries.)

Subsequently, in 1993, Jack bought an iceboat and was thereby safeguarded from falling from the sky. Hand-crafted in Ompah, Ontario, the twelve-foot-long wooden class boat was patterned after the DN or *Detroit News* boats built as part of a competition to see who could build the fastest one-man ice boat. With a sixteen-foot mast and a tapered area upon which to lie, boats such as these have been clocked at over sixty miles per hour. Pierre Berton's book, *Winter*, has a photo taken in 1915 of similar, although larger boats that people used to take from Toronto Island to the mainland. Jack and Thom sailed the boat for the first time at Norway Lake on Christmas day in 1994 when he was seventy-two years old.

Some may say that Jack allowed his appreciation for cars to morph into a post-mid-life crisis. Well into his seventies, he's enjoyed driving a series of convertible sports cars. He had a 1978 MGB in British racing green and subsequently a bright red 1991 Mazda Miata. He still has the Miata (as of summer 2001) that he uses for summer driving around town, plus he has a late-model Honda Accord for longer trips and winter driving.

One of the highlights of the past ten years has been the Lockwoods' ongoing involvement with the annual Lumber Baron Festival that celebrates Renfrew's heritage as a lumber-producing town. At noon hour every day of the week-long festival, Jack fires a gun in front of the town hall and makes announcements to the assembled crowd. It is this that lead him to being proclaimed the town crier in 1990. When asked how he knows what to say after the opening "Oye! Oye!" he replies, "Agnes and I work on what to say, depending on the occasion. In the current message, I talk about the Millionaires hockey team. With the cannon, and all, I just started doing it."

And if this caused any consternation among the mandarins at the town hall, what could they do but embrace these antics? The cannon, the costume, the pomp, circumstance and bombast of it all. The history of town criers goes back to the Spartan runners in the early Greek Empire. As the custom spread to northern Europe, the position of town crier became important in the community. The town crier was the king's representative and, as such, was protected. The town may have wanted to halt the kaboom of the Lockwood cannon (and of others), and they may have wanted to preclude adults dressing up in costume except for Halloween and Christmas. However, with the wisdom of city fathers, they welcomed the histrionics and history.

And then, when the Royal Bank presented Jack with a brass bell to summon the public, what is it they say about you can't fight city hall or big business?

Oye! Oye! Renfrew, let it flourish!

Out on the First Concession

by Wes Bomhower

It was finally summer, the grass was lush and green, and Alphonse let the horses out to cavort around the small meadow beside the barn. They munched on the new grass, a welcome change in diet from long winter months with dry hay and oats as their sustenance.

Alphonse Lafarge, with his good wife and family, lived just across the road, and their house and outbuildings were like a second home to me. They kept three horses, a dozen or so cows, and some pigs and chickens. Two of the girls, about my age, were also very pretty.

Mrs. Lafarge was a tiny woman. Though not a licensed veterinarian, she nevertheless took pride in diagnosing certain ailments in animals when the situation arose. Her success rate was above average.

On this early June evening as the horses tossed their heads and cantered about trying to ward off the many mosquitoes, Old Jim, the oldest horse, stumbled and fell. Though he didn't appear to be hurt, he seemed unable to rise to his feet again. Alphonse, ever watchful of his animals, tried to prod Old Jim to life, but to no avail. Turning to me he said, "Buckshot, would you get your father and big brother to come over?" I rather liked that nickname, it made me feel older than my eight years, so I hustled to do his bidding.

Dad, Everett, and I returned to the pasture where two other neighbours who had been summoned arrived also. Together with Alphonse the men practically lifted Old Jim to his feet. Jim was a bit unsteady, but soon was cropping grass again. The men chatted a bit then suddenly Old Jim's legs gave out again. No amount of coaxing or lifting could make him stand this time. Mrs. Lafarge who had been watching from the house came on the scene.

For the life of me I can't recall her diagnosis of Old Jim's ailment, but she did recommend plenty of heat. "Get those three cast-iron skillets from the back kitchen," she ordered one of the older girls. "Garfield, you fetch some of that dry oak from the woodshed," and her teenage son went grudgingly to do her bidding.

Soon the big wood range was fired up and the skillets were nearly red-hot. Mrs. Lafarge, with a metal coat hanger through the handle of one skillet, came dashing into the pasture. She applied the pan to Old Jim's abdomen and the smell of burning hair and flesh filled the air.

Old Jim moaned and flailed his legs about but made no effort to rise. A second skillet was applied with a little more moaning and flailing, then Jim lifted his head to see a third skillet coming, and this one red-hot. The horse made a valiant effort to rise to avoid the skillet and Mrs. Lafarge shouted, "Lookit Alphonse, he's getting better already, he's trying to get up. All you men give him a lift now." With a little help Old Jim was upright once more, his belly still smoldering.

It was now twilight, and after getting the horse back to his stall, everyone returned home leaving Old Jim to contemplate the hazards of his malady, whatever it was.

Alas, the effort of rising one last time proved too much and Old Jim lay dead in his box stall next morning. Mrs. Lafarge had found a cure but lost a patient.

The Gathering of the McNab Settlers

by Neil Stewart

As boys, my younger brother and I were privileged to learn a few lessons of local history at the knee of our grandfather. Grandpa was a livestock dealer and a long-time politician. He knew every lot and concession in McNab Township, the families who settled there, the successes they enjoyed, the tragedies they suffered. He was often treated more as a friend than a businessman or politician. His own grandfather had been one of the first to settle in the township, and his father's older brothers had often told him stories of the early years.

As we drove around the roads of McNab Township in the late 1940s and early '50s, Dad or Grandpa would often point out landmarks to us. That would lead to a story or tale—sometimes humorous, sometimes serious. These stories sparked an interest in local history. One concerned the great gathering of settlers at Allan Stewart's farm.

It happened in 1840. After years of persecution, inability to get title to their lots, and frustration from repeated unsuccessful requests to the government to investigate the administration of their township, the settlers resolved once more to try lifting the burdens placed on them by the incompetent and vindictive Archibald McNab.

Dugald C. McNab wrote that it was a balmy, June day when the settlers from every corner of McNab Township made their way to Balmer Island in the Flat Rapid Settlement at Lot 13, Concession 7—the centre of the township. Here they gathered at the clearance of Allan Stewart. Murdock McDonald of the Goshen Settlement piped steadily from early morning until the assembly was called to order. There was much debate. Some of those who had suffered greatly under the Chief's administration wanted severe action taken—even suggesting that the McNab be seized, tried, and executed on the spot. But these were the few. Most of the leaders in the community spoke with determination that they must once more try to use all constitutional means to bring about justice.

They were Presbyterians mostly, with a few Catholics and some followers of the Methodist and Baptist sects. These men were strong, physically and mentally. They had left their native land. They had cleared the forest to build farms and raise families. Some of them had endured unnecessary poverty. They had also survived fifteen years and more under the hands of a petty tyrant, yet most of them were more successful in terms of personal wealth and security than they had been back in their beloved Scotland. If only they could achieve that final step of independence. However, they were not about to do anything rash, to squander what they had achieved by sheer hard work.

So while the women prepared a picnic lunch from baskets carried to the site, and the children shyly made acquaintances with new playmates, 135 men talked and argued and debated the course of action they must take. At last it was agreed that they would send Dugald C. McNab to meet with Lord Sydenham, Governor-in-Chief of Canada, in Toronto. An amount of money was raised on the spot and more was pledged for the future to meet the expenses of Mr. McNab. A petition, dated June 3, 1840, and signed by 133 of those men in attendance, was drafted for presentation to Sydenham. By mid-afternoon, the settlers were wending their way back to their clearings in Burnstown, Canaan, Goshen, Sand Point, and the newly named Arnprior, and across the Madawaska to the White Lake country.

For the next three years, there were many legal battles and a report by the Chief. Finally, in 1843, it all ended with the McNab leaving the township forever. However, it still took many years of effort before the settlers received clear title to their lots even though some of the earliest settlers had completed all settlement duties as early as 1828.

By 1845, new settlers from Scotland were moving into the area, and names such as Lochwinnoch and New Glasgow were being used to identify settlements in the township. By the late nineteenth century, McNab Township was the largest in population and assessment in the County of Renfrew.

Some years after the township was incorporated, a new town hall was erected on Lot 13, Concession 6—near the site of that early historic gathering. A few years later, a post office was granted for the area and named Stewartville in honour of Allan Stewart.

That action by the settlers on a hot, June day in 1840 was a lesson in participatory democracy that should never be forgotten.

"Dear Lenny;
You see I have followed your advice. And I am happy to state that the Laird of Macnab was restored the dignity of his clan. The most proper reception greeted myself and my counsellor and I have pleasure in reporting that the Governor of Canada has very properly invited me to take possession of a large territory, to administer it on behalf of the government, and to lead there so many of people as are willing to come. I shall be writing to you in some weeks to aske you to act as agent for their transportation, etc., and will give you further news. I will not rest content until I see around me my people, on their own land, under the control of their own Chief."

(Signed)
MacNab

— From Archibald MacNab to his clansman, Dr. Hamilton at Lenny, Scotland, after MacNab successfully petitioned for a township on the Ottawa River covering 81,000 acres, October 1823.

"I, Archibald McNab, of McNab, do hereby locate you, James Carmichael, upon the rear half of the Sixteenth Lot of the Eleventh Concession of McNab, upon the following terms and conditions, that is to say: I hereby bind

myself, my heirs and successors, to give you the said land free of any quit rent for three years from this date, as also to procure you a patent for the same at your expense, upon your having done the settlement duties and your granting me a mortgage upon said lands, that you will yearly hereafter pat to me, my heirs and successors for ever one bushel of wheat or Indian corn, or oats of like value, for every cleared acre upon the said Lot of Land in name of Quit Rent for the same, in the month of January each year. Your subscribing to these conditions being binding upon you to fulfil the terms thereof. Signed and sealed by us at Kenell Lodge, this twelfth day of August, 1825."

(Signed) Archibald McNab
James Carmichael

— One of the agreements signed between McNab and his tenants, James Carmichael. He also signed similar agreements with Donald Fisher, Peter Campbell, Peter Drummond, James Robertson, Alexander MacNab, James McFarlane, Duncan Campbell, James McDonald, Donald McNaughton, Joh McDiermid, John McIntyre, Peter McIntyre, Don McIntyre, James McLaurin, Peter MacMillan, James Stories, James McFarlane (Crief), Alexander Miller, Malcolm McLaren, and Colin McCaul.

Old-Time Stuff—Recollections of Charles Naughton, Calabogie

originally printed in The Ottawa Citizen, *July 11, 1923*

My father Bartholomew Naughton came out from Tarbot, Limerick County, Ireland, and my mother Mary Vaughan from Glin, Limerick County. They were married and lived in London, England, for some years before coming out to Canada in 1843. They came up to what was called at that time "The Front," namely Perth, and after remaining in Perth for a short time, decided to take up farming. It seems strange that they left the good lands between here and Perth and picked on stony land. The reasons given for making such a choice were that the good land was low and wet, and that the high dry land was to be preferred. This could be accounted for by reason that the big trade in those days was the potash industry and it did not matter so much what the land was as long as it was dry and the wood could be converted. In addition to this my father had learned that there had been a settlement of people from his own county Limerick that was called Ashdad and Mount St. Patrick, and naturally to be with and near his own. In course of time, he got his land picked out and got his belongings in, and as was usual with early settlers, built a temporary shanty.

A Sample of Early Settlers' Hard Luck

An unfortunate accident occurred shortly after they had moved into their new home. There were no stoves in the country at that time and cooking was done on an open fire outside, or those who had built for far enough ahead, had an open fireplace in the house. In this case, we just got in and were cooking for the time being on an open fire outside. This day after dinner, the family went down to the meadow to cut some hay—this was in about the month of August—and while away they had not taken precautions to put out the fire before leaving. The result was while away a wind blew up and burned the shanty and all their possessions, leaving them with only the clothes on their backs. This was a terrible plight to be in. Old Country people with absolutely no experience of bush life, such as it was at that time, and neighbours who were almost as badly off as themselves.

Walked to Montreal

However, they struggled through and my father wrote his brother in London telling him of his plight and he remitted him some money. And when it arrived, he had to walk to Montreal to get it. Some walk. But people in those days did not think anything of walking fifty or a hundred miles.

Hard Going

We used to have to carry wheat first to White Lake, fifteen miles away. One would take out whatever he could carry on his back in wheat and bring it back in flour. There would be four or five weeks in the year when there would be no flour to be had. As a result, no bread. Just imagine how people would feel today if they had to go four or five weeks without bread or cereals and substitute potatoes for bread.

In order to hurry the flour along, it was always the custom to let a small piece of wheat stand just a few days longer until it got good and ripe, then cut it and thrash it, and expose it to the air and sun for two or three weeks until it got good and hard, so that it could be ground.

All the milling in those days was done on stones, and if the wheat was not good and hard and dried, it would clog up the stones and you would not get the same amount of flour from your wheat. In addition, the miller disliked very much having to clean his stone after having put through a batch of soft wheat.

Getting Closer

Latterly in about '52, a mill was built at Calabogie down about where the present O'Brien Power House is located. It was taken away in 1871, the year of the high water, and never rebuilt. One of the old stones may be seen at the bottom of the river. It was built by one Cummings and was later bought out by Hunters who were United Empire Loyalists.

Humorous Story of a Christening
I remember well my mother telling the experience she had when my older brother William was baptized eighty-one years ago. They had got word that a missioner (*sic*), Father McNulty, would be at Calabogie Lake at a certain date, and when the time came, my mother and Mrs. Murphy and a Mrs. Hayley set out to go to the lake, which was four miles away, to have the child christened. The only way that they could reach the lake was by going through the bush and making their way by following the blazes on the trees. They started out in the morning and all went very well until they discovered they had lost the blaze.

Mrs. Murphy and Mrs. Hayley told my mother to stay where she was with the baby and that they would go and find the blaze, which they proceeded to do. But as they were so long away, my mother became very fearful and laid the babe down at the foot of a tree and went off to find her companions. After a lot of wandering and shouting, she succeeded in finding them and locating the blazed trail. But now they found the blaze, they had lost child. I'm told that my mother was almost frantic and almost out of her mind. But they finally found the babe and proceeded on their way and had it baptized at the Mission.

Pathetic Tale of the Hungry Winter
The end of 1869 and the beginning of 1870 was known as "The Hungry Winter." Very little snow fell until February 2, 1870. Then snow fell to a depth of thirty-eight inches in three days, and it kept snowing until there was six feet of snow on the level. In places it had drifted twenty feet high. The result was that it was almost impossible to get in and out, and things were at a standstill. The snow remained on the ground until the first of May. One could go anywhere on the crust during the month of April.

Dear Hay
On Easter Sunday of that year, I had occasion to go out to the lake and took across the country on the crust. At that time, the snow was still so deep that no fences were to be seen anywhere. Hay was scarce and sold at $50 a ton, and as the winter progressed, the price to $100 a ton. The hotelkeeper named Robert Miller at Dacre offered $100 a ton for hay and could not get any sellers for that price, for the reason that there was none to be had in the country.

All of the hay and oats had been bought up in the early part of the season by the lumbermen at $30 a ton for hay and 75¢ a bushel for oats, and taken into the lumber camps. This left the country with a very small stock of fodder. And, owing to the deep snow, it was practically impossible to bring in supplies of this kind into the outlying districts. Horses that were in the lumber camps all winter and had returned to their homes in the springtime died by the score on the road home, as in the country through which they were passing, nothing could be had.

Died from U.S. Corn
It is true that they were enabled to get some American corn. This seemed to only make matters worse as the horses seemed to get sick and die when they were fed with it. As the supplies of hay and straw ran out early in the season, the cattle were fed browsing principally hemlock branches. They fared very well on this during the cold weather of the winter, but as soon as the weather began to get warmer, they did not do so well. And, as there was no other feed or source of supply, they also died by the score. Sugar was selling at 10 pence per pound, tea at four shillings and tobacco at 90¢ and flour $14 per barrel. Very little sugar was bought in those times, as everyone made their own maple sugar and every home would possibly have a couple of hundred pounds of maple sugar made up for the year's use. Fruit of all kinds was always preserved in maple sugar, and it was also used in place of cane sugar.

No Working Hours
Talk about working hours in the old times. It amuses me to hear men object to working nine hours per day, when we in the old times worked from daylight to dark.

Men Had to be Men in Those Old Days
I remember well on one drive of timber which we took off the Madawaska River to Quebec running our cribs from what was then called Birchtown, latterly Skead's Mills and now called Westboro.[1] First thing in the morning, we would get through the timber slide. If we were unlucky, we would run into the pig pen, so called because it was a very strong eddy, which is now known as Nepean Bay. Once you got into this with a crib of timber, you were likely to row around for some hours before you got out.

After coming through the slide, we would row down, tie up at the foot of the locks, and walk back to Westboro for breakfast.

I wonder how our modern young men would like to do this for an appetizer. Most of the times it was after dark before we finished our day's work. And we were always out before daylight. Yes, men had to be men in those days.

Girls Read This and Then Wonder
Quite a number of girls in these parts went to work in surrounding towns, and I remember well

some girls who were working in Arnprior, twenty-nine miles distant. As a rule, they had one Sunday off a month and after supper on Saturday evening, they would start and walk for home, twenty-five to thirty miles away, and this would bring them home. Sometimes in the small hours of the morning, and after resting a few hours, they would then go to church seven miles away. One of the reasons for going to church would be to meet old friends. They would get back from church, say about two o'clock, have dinner, and possibly around five o'clock, tea, and then walk back to Arnprior and get there in time for Monday morning's work.

Story of Some Early Indians

Yes, we had Indians in those parts in the early days. In fact, we had many Indians, but they all seem to have died off or been gathered into the Reserve at Golden Lake. There was an Indian camping ground at Calabogie Lake at the mouth of Consta Creek. I can remember well the Indians in the spring leaving to go away up the rivers and creeks for the summer and coming down again and taking their trips down the Ottawa River, trading backwards and forwards, coming back again in the winter and dispersing throughout the woods, generally locating where food could be had readily, especially near a deer yard. Sometimes, they would run short of food and would come around to the settlers and would trade mitts and moccasins, and whatever things they would make up for whatever we could spare. Sometimes it would be potatoes, turnips, or whatever we had. They always seemed to be very grateful. Other times of the year when they had food to spare they would come around with fish or game to repay the kindness done them when they were in need.

Some years ago I found an Indian relic, an old pestle made of stone, evidently dating from the time when Indians had nothing else but stone weapons. This stone club was used for beating, pounding or crushing, and I still have it in my possession.

Frank Partridge was Some Runner

We had runners in those days, too. Talk about Nurmi[2] or Longboat,[3] but Frank Partridge, an Indian, who was in his prime in about the '60s was a marvel of speed and endurance. He was about six feet tall, thin, but well proportioned and straight as an arrow. One of his favourite pastimes was hunting and he would get on the trail of a deer and follow it continuously until he killed it. I remember on one occasion his starting a deer at Shamrock and running it a distance of fifteen miles and killing it with a stick in Grassy Bay on Calabogie Lake.

"It took just three minutes to slice six logs and spew out one thousand feet of choice one-inch by twelve-inch stock. Two crack men kept those saws clear. Stripped to the waist the two 'tailers,' buoyed by a fresh quid of stag and standing behind the gates containing the saws, slung that soggy stock to rollers before the next avalanche swamped them. On, the endless stream of boards rolled to trimmers and cullers, then at the end of the production chain 'frame loaders' stacked them high on horse-drawn lorries to be trotted a quarter of a mile down the echoing plank gangway to the big sorting table. A man who could say, 'I tailed the gates,' or 'I loaded frames' needed no other recommendation. He had to be a good man."

— T.C. Mulvihill, millworker at McLachlin's No. 3 Mill, Arnprior, 1917–25.

Indian was Sore

I remember another time quite well when I was nearly shooting him. It was in the fall of the year and I was out towards Snake Lake when suddenly I heard a hound barking as if it was after a deer. Knowing the country well, I hurried to the runway and the deer would have to take. I stood on the runway quite a while waiting for the time, when suddenly I saw something moving in the woods. I up with my rifle ready to shoot, when lo, instead of the deer followed by the hound, it was Partridge. It seems the deer had passed the runway before I got there and Lizzie, his squaw, was a little further down the lake. But she had missed the deer. He was very wrathy when he learned the deer had got away.

An Indian Runner versus a Horse

I remember another occasion. It was at Opeongo, which was then called Harty's, which was five miles distant from Renfrew. One Martin Mulvihill had one of the finest saddle horses in that part of the country and Partridge challenged him in these words: "I'll run you and your horse to Renfrew for the fun of it." The challenge was taken up by Mulvihill and race was immediately started. The mare had the best of Partridge for the first mile or so, after which Partridge began to hold his own with her. But on the last two miles, he drew away from her and left her far behind. As the mare and rider were coming into Renfrew, Partridge, to celebrate, was standing on his head on a big rock.

Made Mr. Partridge Pay for his Drinks

I also remember one spring on a drive at Dacre, we had Partridge give an exhibition of how fast he could run. We would send him up the road, say two or three hundred yards, and tell him, now if you can run this in so many seconds, we will give you a drink. He would go up the road to the starting point and come back down in most magnificent bursts of speed. And there is no doubt that he wold have done the distance in the time allotted him, but he was told that he was not running fast enough, and he would have to run over again. Partridge would go up the road again and come back at a greater speed.

Kidded Him

He would be again told that he was just not making the required time. Back he went for a third time, and it would do you good to see how fast he could run, because he certainly came tearing down that road at a great rate of speed, and as the men thought he had run enough for their entertainment, he was told that he had made the required time and to come in and have a drink.

I have read with interest accounts of other writers of Joe Montferrand,[4] the champion fighter of Ottawa, but we had men in these parts that could handle him. Montferrand's great offensives were his feet. He fought well with his feet, but when it came to meeting some of our stalwarts, who could use their hands, Mr. Montferrand was *hors de combat*.

---

[1]Now part of Ottawa.

[2]Pavlo Nurmi (1897–1973). Known as the Flying Finn, he dominated long-distance running in the 1920s, during which decade he won nine gold medals at three Olympic Games and set numerous world records.

[3]Tom Longboat (1886–1949). An Onondaga, he was one of the world's premier marathon runners in the decade preceding the First World War. He reached the height of his fame after winning the 1907 Boston Marathon. As a professional, he went on to numerous victories in long distance races.

[4]Joseph Montferrand (1802–64) (aka Big Joe Mufferaw). A legendary log-driver and heroic defender of the rights of the Canadiens on the Ottawa River in the early years of the lumber trade, his feats have become the subject of many tall tales.

Lads

by Garry Ferguson

The black car turned off the township road and slunk down the hill toward me as I was unhitching the team from the haymower at noon. A column of dust spewed up behind it and hung in the cloudless sky, like the smoke mushroom over a bush fire.

Must be some of those city sports from out front, I thought. They're always looking for some place to fish right out of their cars.

"Afternoon," the driver said as he brought the vehicle to a stop beside me.

I took my hat off, hunched down and peered through the opened window. A young woman in shorts sat beside him. Three little fellows stared wide-eyed at me from the rear seat.

"Gidday, gidday, folks," I answered. "Hot weather we're havin', eh."

"Yessir. Certainly is," the driver said. "Great for travelling. Drove all the way from Toronna this morning. We're—ah—looking for a man named McGregor—George McGregor. Moved to this part of the country a few years back. We wondered if you might know him. Where we could find him maybe."

"Well now," I said. "You're a helluva long way from home already and it's only dinner time. George McGregor—hmm." I swung my hat to drive off some flies which had been attracted to the gathering and tried to recall the name. "Sounds familiar, but—he don't live close around. Come to think of it now, there is a lad. Moved in over by—ah—"

"Oh no," he interjected. "This is no lad—"

"Thought you said the name was George." I interrupted his interruption. "If it's George, it's gotta be a lad. All the Georges I ever hearda were lads."

"This guy's an old man—my grandfather's brother."

"Then he's at least a fairly old lad," I assured him. "What d' ya figure it takes to be a lad where you come from?"

"Well . . . I dunno." He seemed to ponder my question. "I suppose—a boy."

"A boy you say? Can't argue with you there. A boy's a lad for sure, but we call all our fellas boys around here. From the cradle all the way to old age dottiness. Depends on how you're talkin' and who you're talkin' to, but mostly they're all lumped together."

"As lads?"

"No. Boys."

"Oh, I see." The man's face wrinkled into a smile. "You've got many categories of boys, but they're all lads just the same."

"Nope. A boy's a boy. Could be any age, like I said. They all eventually get to be allota kinds of lads, though, if they live long enough, eh. All the way from wee little lads to real old lads."

"Ah yes." The man dropped his smile and wrinkled his forehead. "What would I be then?"

In spite of a few grey hairs in his blonde sideburns and crow's feet at the corners of his eyes, he couldn't have been much over thirty. His face was smooth and lean. No long hairs grew in his ears.

"Hmm." I tried to make up my mind. "You look pretty much like an ordinary lad—or maybe even a middle-aged lad. Now take me, eh. I'm one of your fairly old lads. Sounds to me like your grandfather's brother might be up around there, too."

"Uncle George's in his eighties—or maybe nineties," he said thoughtfully.

"Oh! Then he's an old lad for damned sure," I informed him. "Can't be the lad I was gonna tell you about."

"An old lad," he repeated. "Okay. Now, we . . ." he swung his head toward the rear seat. "We have three boys here—from three to twelve. What sort of lads are they?"

"Well—I can't exactly say off hand, but it looks t' me like you got, probly a wee lad, a little lad, and a young lad. They'd all have to get to be fairly young lads before they could get to be just lads. Then they'd be set for quite awhile, y'see, becoz lad covers a lot of a fella's age."

"Right. I understand now. So my great-uncle's an old lad."

"Yyaah," I said triumphantly. "You got 'er now. Sorry I can't help youse, but the wife'd be glad to set a few extra places if you'd like to come on up to the house and sit in to dinner."

They both thanked me "so much," but said they hoped to find a nice place to eat a lunch that they had in the trunk. Then they left.

I watched the car climb back up the hill. Odd conversation, I thought, but they seemed like good people. A fine family. A nice lad.

Prize-Winning Cucumber

by Season Osborne

Verlie Mackie was amongst the 27,000 visitors at the 141st Renfrew Agricultural Fair that trooped past the displays of plump red tomatoes, waxed rutabagas, Spanish onions, bunched carrots—and one gargantuan cucumber. At an impressive twenty-three inches, it put all the piddling foot-long cukes to shame, and had received the virtually uncontested first prize of five dollars.

Verlie would've given it no more than an admiring glance if the loud fellow behind her hadn't scoffed that it was "more'n likely some overgrown zucchini." Verlie, an ardent vegetable grower herself, leaned into the chicken wire display case to verify this. She could see the little bumps on its green skin where the pricklies had been rubbed off. No, this was undoubtedly an extraordinarily large cucumber.

Verlie then read the tag attached to the blue ribbon:

Exhibit — Cucumber: 23 inches,
4 pounds, 3 ounces

Exhibitor — E. Stewart

E. Stewart! Edna and Alf Stewart lived two farms over and had been good neighbours for over thirty years. She and Edna often exchanged recipes, borrowed an egg or a cup of sugar now and then, and were members of the White Lake Women's Institute. They both also had green thumbs.

Their gardens were common topics of conversation. They passed many winter afternoons ruminating over copious cups of tea about what to order from the seed catalogues. Once the seeds were planted, they made regular tours of each other's garden, oohing and aahing over the progress of the seedlings. They commiserated about slug problems, experimented with possible remedies, and congratulated each other when the vegetables emerged unscathed in late June.

Yet, not once all summer had Edna Stewart said anything about a prize cucumber. Not one word. And just last week, they had spent a great deal of time discussing which jelly recipe she should submit to the Renfrew Fair. All the while Edna had kept mum about her vegetable entry.

So, seeing this blue-ribboned cucumber had taken Verlie aback. She had grown some fine cucumbers herself, and wouldn't be surprised if that very cucumber had sprung from the seeds she had given Edna a couple of years ago. It could very well be the grandson of one of her own cucumbers. Verlie decided to say nothing about having seen it at the fair. She felt it was up to Edna to bring the subject up. She could've been hurt by the whole thing, but felt she was bigger than that. The topic was never discussed.

Anyway, she certainly hadn't, by any means, let the episode influence her decision to add more sheep-dip top-dressing to her row of cucumbers the following spring. So it was rather a pleasant surprise, as she was hauling the garden hose down between the rows of shallots, to find an exceptionally long cucumber protruding from the mass of verdant foliage.

Verlie hurried back to the house to retrieve the cloth measuring tape from her sewing basket. Carefully, so as not to sever the vegetable from its umbilical cord to the plant, she measured the cucumber's length and girth: nineteen inches by eight inches. It was indeed, the daddy of cucumbers. And this was only the beginning of August. By fair time, it would be a record-breaker.

Verlie checked her giant cuke daily. She bought a special fertilizer from Home Hardware and twice a week ardently doused the plant. It worked. The cucumber had grown to twenty-one inches in length by the Friday of the following week.

She made extra effort to pull out the Scotch grass and clumps of dandelion leaves from around the plant so that the weeds wouldn't absorb any of the essential nutrients. She also picked the nearby smaller cukes so that the plant would channel all of its energy into the big one. Consequently, she spent days tediously canning three dozen jars of bread and butter pickles.

When the mercury rose above ninety degrees Fahrenheit, Verlie opened her red umbrella over the cucumber plant to act as a parasol, shading it from the midday sun. The last thing she needed was the cucumber to yellow before she picked it. And it did look pretty from her kitchen window, like a rare, giant, red poppy springing up in the midst of her garden.

August was a long, hot, dry month, and Verlie prayed each time she turned on the sprinkler that this wouldn't be the year her well ran dry. She'd toss and turn at night, waking in a heart-pounding sweat from nightmares about marauders sneaking into gardens and picking all the produce.

Edna would call up most afternoons, and they would have a lovely chat about earwigs and scabs. Verlie eagerly discussed the powdery mildew on her Bright Lights Swiss char, but veered away from the topic of cucumbers. She thought, "two can play that game."

The last week of August, Verlie drove her rusty Ford LTD to the fairgrounds. In the office, the secretary hunched over a clunky typewriter and dangled a cigarette from her mouth, her yellow hair in a fog of smoke.

Verlie nervously exchanged a five-dollar bill for the vegetable prize list handed to her, and filled out the entry form. She was past the point of no return. Her cucumber would be exhibited as the largest cucumber ever grown in the county. Verlie was sure of it. Then, with great self-control, she left the office without asking the secretary if Edna Stewart had entered another cucumber.

The morning of the day the exhibits were to be submitted, Verlie was up at six rummaging through her bag of scrap material to line the basket she would take her cucumber to the fair in. Presentation was everything. She found a remnant of the shiny, red satin she'd made a bridesmaid's dress out of years ago. She carefully ironed, then folded the satin into the bottom of the basket. She had learned a thing or two from that Martha Stewart show.

Finally, the moment of reckoning came and she solemnly walked between the rows of recently debeaned plants to the cucumber patch. She closed the red umbrella and the sun gleamed off the cucumber's dark green skin. It had reached a fantastic twenty-six inches in length. With scissors shaking nervously, she snipped the stem. Gingerly lifting the precious cucumber, she weighed it in her hands. 'At least six pounds,' she thought smugly. She tenderly laid it in its bed of satin and carried it to the car. She even extended the seat belt over the basket as an extra precaution.

She'd stop first at Fred's Gas and General Store, where they had a reliable scale.

She kept well under the speed limit on the main road with her precious cargo. The driver of the car behind leaned rudely on the horn as she cautiously made the turn into Fred's parking lot. Verlie undid the seat belt from around the basket and carried it into the store. The bell over the door announced her entrance.

Fred senior was shoving red sides of beef into the walk-in freezer at the back. He waved and she waited at the counter with her basket. "What you got in there, a puppy?" he hollered up to her. Verlie was too nervous to smile back. He came up wiping his red hands on his stained apron, looked in and whistled. "That for the fair?" She nodded and Fred gently lifted the cucumber out and set it on the scale. The needle sprang into motion. "Looks like it'll easily be over four," he said. "Sure is bigger than that one last year that Ernie Stewart won the blue ribbon for."

She was about to ask if he meant Edna rather than Ernie Stewart, when in marched the two Crozier brats letting the door bang behind them. The vibration of the slam sent the cucumber rocking on the scale. It took only a fraction of a second—though to Verlie it happened in slow motion. The next thing she knew, the big green cylinder rolled off the scale and disappeared over the counter. There was a dull thud as it bounced off the cash register, a pause, then a hollow smack as it hit the floor.

Fred stared down at his feet and Verlie stared dully at the empty scale. Without a word Fred bent down. He came back up with three green pieces: two ends and a middle. He handed them apologetically across the counter. Verlie dumped the pieces into her basket and looked down at them, their bared white circle of seeds naked against the red satin.

It started in her stomach, burbled up her throat, and burst out between her teeth: a high, thin laugh, bordering on hysteria. It tumbled out uncontrollably until soon Fred was chuckling and wiping his eyes along with her. Finally, Verlie sighed, picked up her basket and took her broken cucumber home to make relish.

The Eye of the Beholder

by Phoneas Barbutt

The long path that winter had laid to my door had seemed endless. But spring was now upon us and, with it, the promise of another new fishing season. We excitedly planned our first fishing trip. We would be challenging the abundant trout that is found in many of the lakes and streams of Renfrew County.

In my youth, we fractured the English language with our declaration of, "Spring has come, the grass has risen—It's time for us to get out fishin'!" It was our expression of the significance of what transforms mankind from a dormant existence during the long winter into the vibrant beings of spring. We were eager to share a place in an invigorating new surrounding. All of spring's armament of bubbling new life and vitality helped to make this transformation a reality.

Now it was time again for man to pit himself against all of the elements he will encounter while fishing. He loads himself with every conceivable bit of gear he can find and assures himself that he cannot possibly fail with all of the guarantees that come with his purchases. Prepared, he trucks off to his favourite haunts without regard to whose side Mother Nature will be on—man or fish's. Nothing will detract the average Izaak Waltons of the world in their determination to simply show up, conquer, and return home laden with the spoils of victory.

Every fisherman goes through this discipline, having rehearsed it mentally many times during those long wintry days. So, surely, by Opening Day, the planning will simply fall into place. As easily as they did in his dreams.

Opening Day finally did arrive. Dawn broke with the beauty and serenity that only this time of day can bring. I had eagerly checked all of my gear the night before, laying it out in a systematic order of importance. However, I would double-check before heading out to ensure that *nothing* was missing or had been left to chance. As I waited for my fishing companions to show, I became aware of an increasing level of excitement and anticipation for what would lie ahead.

The early morning rising and break from my normal routine was a combined pleasure. The usual demands on my time would not be missed today. What a blessing it was to escape, even for one day. A joy magnified by the fact that I would spend the day with my most ideal companions—my sons!

I rediscovered the fun and excitement of the early morning pick-up. The trip to the lake was mingled with good-natured barbs, offered by each to the others in jest. Most centred on each one's inabilities and shortcomings in the world of fishing. The tripped passed much too quickly.

On arriving at our destination, and while my sons were unloading our boat and gear, my attention was drawn to the only other people there. A young father and his small son were attempting to lure that first trout of the day. My mind flashed back to the time when I was that young father and the small son was any one of my own. A lifetime of experiences flashed through my mind. I could see those good memories as clearly as if they were today. Then suddenly, they were gone and the magic of that brief moment was lost in the reality of the here and now. That experience was the first of several to occur on this outing, and it encouraged me to look beyond the obvious.

The lake was calm. A brilliant clear sky cast a blanket of blue over a green shoreline of towering pines. I thought it odd that I could not remember the sky being so glorious before. Nor could I recall the statuesque pines appearing to stand on guard for us. The screeches of a pair of mating blackbirds as they darted amongst the trees gathering nesting materials challenged the serenity. Small aquatic insects scurried across the flat surface of the lake, busy with their own lives, needs, and survival. A blue heron stood motionless in his domain of reeds and shallows. Another of Nature's sentinels. For although he stood completely still—some would even say asleep—a closer look revealed piercing eyes and a rapier-like bill, both trained on the many small creatures that darted within his reach.

The warmth of the quickly rising sun reminded our bodies of how little sleep we'd had the night before. The drone of electric trolling motors added to the spell that had us standing in awe of the beauty of our surroundings. Then my son yelled, "Fish on!" breaking our trance.

"Battle stations" seems the best way to describe the sudden coming to life of our crew. Tackle boxes were knocked over, drink and bait were spilled, and nets mislaid in the scramble to get ready for action.

Amidst all the confusion, I had another flashback to when I was a young boy fishing with my father. I was determined to show that I could manage that rod and reel, and put on my own bait. The image then changed to reveal my son with that same look of determination on his face. I have no doubts that he, too, has witnessed this look in his own children.

As we fished and continued the good-natured barbs on catching the "big one," I absorbed the best of two worlds—today's reality and yesterday's memory.

The sun had reached its peak and we realized that, unfortunately, it was time to call it a day. What a time we had had, and what an assortment of precious memories had been mixed in with it. A slight breeze wafted through the treetops, reminding us to "come again, soon—we'll be here."

We headed across the lake towards the sandy beach at my son's cottage where family members were relaxing in the sun's warm rays. Grandchildren cavorted about, busy investigating all the sights and sounds, then ran to witness what they believed would be a truly monstrous trophy fish. They had heard some of the tales of promise made before our trip. Perhaps, in retrospect, the storyteller had distorted some of the facts of previous expeditions, for they were disappointed to discover that the "catch" fell far short of their imagination.

Soon they returned to the important issues of their day: minnows to catch in the shallow waters, bugs and butterflies to chase, and frogs to display in any type of container for all to see.

They are still a little young to understand that neither quality nor size was the most important part of this day. The "catch" had no relevance either now or then. Yet my creel had been full and my limit reached. For I had been given the opportunity to go fishing with my favourite companions in a Renfrew County setting that defies a worthy description. And see many sights that, on this occasion, presented many different meanings to this beholder than I had ever seen before.

Canadian Folk Songs

by Garry Ferguson

A land without song,
Can't stand very long,
When the voice of its people is dead.
— Tom Connors

While listening to good old CBC Radio, as I often do when I'm within broadcast range of Ottawa, I heard an over-the-phone interview that left me hyperventilating and blaming the wax in my ears for playing tricks with my hearing.

A man representing a museum was being questioned about the museum's plan to recreate an early Canadian country fair for the public. When asked about music, he said that it was on the program—mostly American—like Stephen Foster compositions. During my ensuing semiconscious state—brought on by inhaling my morning coffee while hyperventilating—I could swear I heard the bones of my ancestors rattle as they did somersaults in their graves.

For more than a century, *les voyageurs* and the lumbermen, each group possessing an incredible folk song tradition, passed within virtual hailing distance of where the man worked. The shanty boys carried their music across this country and into the United States during the days when they could get a job in a U.S. lumber camp on the strength of being Canadian. Their music has been collected in places as far away as Texas, Britain, and Australia.

It wasn't only the shanty boys and *voyageurs* who gave us our rich body of folk songs estimated to number in the tens of thousands. As well as songs in the many languages of indigenous peoples, there were in French and English, songs of love, war, murder, cowboys, fishing, farming, and all of the other events that touched the lives of our forebears.

Regardless of language (we even have bilingual songs), traditional Canadian folk music seems to fall into three broad categories: those imported by the early settlers, hybrids or Canadian versions of imports, and songs native to Canada. People such as Kenneth Peacock, Dr. Helen Creighton, Dr. Marius Barbeau, Dr. Roy Mackenzie, Barabara Cass-Beggs, and Edith Fowke dedicated a great deal of their lives to preserving this music from the prairies to Newfoundland. On records and in print, these collections are available to anyone who is interested.

It's true, a few of the old "tragedy" ballads, sung unaccompanied and in minor keys, might not go over too well at a modern rock concert. If the gig was held in Maple Leaf Gardens, the place would be empty somewhere around the forty-seventh verse of the first number. As a kid growing up along the Madawaska in Renfrew County, I used to snicker a bit when old singers spoke the last line of those ballads. I thought they were in a hurry to finish. I didn't realize that they were using a unique technique to announce the end of the performance. In spite of modern trends, this music is still enjoyable. A timeless window on our past, it's Canadian—ours.

We can safely assume that most early Canadian country folk would have had some sort of exposure to music from abroad, including that of Foster, but any depiction of their lives must include *their* music. "The voice," referred to in Tom Connors' song, was very much alive during their time. Its echo can still be heard out along the rural routes.

I'm not sure why we have aspiring historians who can't hear it. I guess we could be kind and blame it on wax in *their* ears.

"There is scarcely a portage, or cleared point, jutting out into the river where you do not meet with wooden crosses, on which are rudely carved the initials of some unfortunate victim of the restless waters. . . . In a prosperous year about ten thousand men are afloat on loose timber, or in frail canoes, and as many as eighty lives have been lost in a single spring. . . . Some of the eddies in high water become whirlpools, tearing a bark canoe into shreds and engulfing every soul in it."

— Thomas C. Keefer, Civil Engineer, to the Mechanics Institute, 1854.

Strange Mists on the Madawaska

by R. Ernest Jukes

"They're makin' the drive!" was the springtime cry as the ice went out of northern rivers in days gone by. From the camboose logging camps along the Madawaska River, hardy Glengarry Scots floated their "sticks" of pine down to the mills on the giant Ottawa. The axemen from our part of Renfrew County went to "shanty" along the early trails, such as the Frontenac Road and Opeongo Line. They cut all winter with axe and cross-cut saw, and then skidded the logs with horses to the frozen water's edge to await the spring thaw. Those gritty rivermen began their treacherous log drive knowing some would never return.

The Madawaska Valley is quite different today. Not the pristine forests of yesterday, but still fine scenery to be sure. Modern highways have made the clear lakes and blue ridges of this handsome area fairly accessible, yet somehow it holds on to its old ways and quaint secrets surprisingly well. One secret, untold till now, has been known to only a few living people and a few . . . well, let's go back a few years.

We three voyageurs had put our canoe into the downstream flow of the Madawaska River just below the falls at Palmer Rapids. Our plan was to take a leisurely trip south for a few days to a picturesque site at some very large rapids located a few miles above Black Donald, an interesting old village built around a graphite mine and named after a dust-covered miner. However, due to the construction of a large electrical generating dam nearby, both the town site and the spectacular rapids are now underwater.

The fishing was excellent along the way as we swam and drifted in the warm July sun. Hit after hit, the smallmouth black bass gave us action as we moved with the current down the historical waterway. It may go without saying we enjoyed a delicious fish fry when we camped that evening, just above the notorious Snake Rapids that had often dashed the rivermen of the past to their deaths.

On the water bright and early the next morning, we carefully negotiated the long series of raging rapids of this dangerous section of river by running from island to island. On one of them, just past Rifle Chute, lay half a Grumman aluminum canoe, torn in two from having its back broken against a boulder. This is a rough, tough, sassy river. Unforgiving and deadly, too, as evidenced by the French names of long-departed souls carved into a large rock on the wooded portage near Slate Falls.

Sketch by R.E. Jukes.

With gear tied in, we shot the rest of the white-water to Griffith Bridge at Highway 41. Following a short portage, we sallied on down along the slow-moving flats just above the old Camel Chute sawmill. We were soon into more bass, as well as some Northerns. "Here's another," Bill hooted as he tied into a good sized bass. The Algonquin natives of the area called the smallmouth Achigan—"the one that fights." How right they were. Inch for inch and pound for pound, they are probably the gamest fish that swims.

We gladly stopped for a well deserved stretch and lunch after running Camel Chute rapids. Here again was another odd name, evidently evolving from the Valley vernacular of Campbell's Chute. A settler had established a sawmill there in the early 1800s.

From the small beach we could see that the river road branched. One to Calabogie and the other leaving the river and going up over the steep hill to my village of Matawatchan. It was there, many years before, that I had chummed up with an older friend, Joe McLaren, a former logger, surveyor and riverman. We must have looked an odd couple as he was almost seventy and I was not quite twelve. Joe taught me how to read whitewater, a lot about the bush, and life in general in his own quiet way.

Continuing our journey, it was an easy run through the Wolf Rapids, moving us ever closer to our destination—the mighty Colton's.
Again a fish smashed the surface, breaking the tranquillity, this time on Rob's line, which trolled a small leopard frog. Lures work, but a frog is often dynamite. The whole strategy of employing a "bug"-type critter is to make it act like the real thing. The closer to natural appearance, the better the chances of fooling a lurking fish.

After going under the old iron bridge, the next half hour of paddling passed quickly. The roar of those grand Colton's—broad rapids with river-wide ripping chutes, dropping in series; perhaps thirty feet or more of rampaging waterfalls—could be heard just around the corner. We slowly stroked up to the rocky shore and landed cautiously at its height. There before us lay a compelling, almost staggering display of glistening rocks and thundering water plunging down, down, down, through the dazzling rainbow mists for the next hundred or more yards.

There were still drill holes for iron stakes in the pink granite where rivermen had tied their booms and large pointer boats filled with supplies. Joe had told me of the many lives lost on these cataracts, and the long days and exhausting physical labour of the log drives. The cooks would go ahead of the drive and set up camp at designated locations, such as this. In their boats, they would carry stoves, tents, pots,

pans, and lots of salt pork, beans, and blackstrap molasses to feed the hungry crew.
We pitched our tent on high ground overlooking the spectacular view and gathered firewood. Then we fried up a pan of flour-dipped bass in bacon drippings, and served them with potatoes and creamed corn to our own hungry crew. The whitewater, rocks, and grassy bank were soon painted in a wash of amber as the red sun set behind the tall pines on the other shore. When the cool of the evening dew settled over us and the embers glowed smaller and smaller, we crawled into our three-man "A" tent. The booming of the rapids became a lullaby, drifting us off to a sound slumber in our comfortable sleeping bags. Or so I thought.

With a sudden start, loud voices awakened me. Not one, but a number of men. Bellowing! I threw open the tent flaps and looked out, while muttering to myself, "Dammit, its three a.m." Who and where, were our annoying nocturnal visitors? I strained my eyes into the inky blackness—no lights, no boats—but again I heard muffled shouts. Slipping into my moccasins, I moved quietly out of the tent toward the shore. Maybe some damn fool fishermen drifted over the rapids in a boat? But at night?

Suddenly I saw them through the rising mists, with moonlight on their backs! There appeared to be men on the river, right at the rapids' edge—with peaveys and pike poles—yelling instructions to one another as they hopped about on the black surface. Then Bill poked his head out of the tent to ask, "Who's hollering?"

Rubbing my eyes in disbelief, I looked again. They were still there—desperately shouting and jumping back and forth on an invisible log jam.

Rob now also inquired from within the tent, "What's the noise out there?"

"Go back to bed," his older brother grumbled.

I blinked again and all was gone! It was quiet, save for the thundering rapids. I immediately returned to my warm bag. After turning and tossing and a lot of wondering, I finally fell back to sleep.

What happened there? Was it a peculiar environmental phenomenon "photographing" a tragedy and exposing it at certain times under correct atmospheric conditions? Apparently, aspects of tragic events, like the Battle of Hastings in eleventh century England, and other authenticated sightings are revealed to spectators again and again. Was this "happening" a trick of nature, resulting from the swirling mists, the moonlight, the noise of the rapids? Or did we somehow delude ourselves, yet without alcohol or other substances to warp our wits. Had we just been over-tired, suffering from too much sun, prone to a vivid imagination? Maybe. But all three of us? You go figure it out. We didn't, nor have we discussed it much between ourselves or anyone else. Who would believe it? It's another secret of the valley. The answer lies only within the strange mists of Colton's on the Madawaska.

For more information on the

COUNTY OF RENFREW

9 International Drive
Pembroke, ON CANADA K8A 6W5
Phone: (613) 735-7288 • Fax (613) 735-2081

or visit our website
www.countyofrenfrew.on.ca

To order more copies of

DRAW UP A CHAIR:

A Treasury of Renfrew County Storytelling

send $19.95 plus $6.00
to cover GST, shipping and handling to: